Reekie's Architectural Drawing

Reekie's Architectural Drawing

Fourth edition

FRASER REEKIE
FRIBA, FRSA, FRTPI, DipArch, DipTP (RIBA)
Chartered Architect, Chartered Town Planner

Fourth Edition revised by

TONY McCARTHY
RIBA, DipRP (Edin) FRSA
Chartered Architect

Edward Arnold
A member of the Hodder Headline Group
LONDON   SYDNEY   AUCKLAND

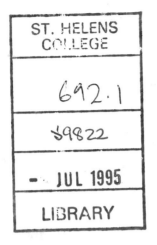
© 1976 R. Fraser Reekie
　1995 Tony McCarthy

First published in Great Britain 1946
Reprinted 1947, 1949, 1952, 1956, 1957, 1959, 1961, 1963, 1965
Second edition 1969
Reprinted 1970, 1971, 1973, 1975
Third edition 1976
Reprinted 1978, 1980 (twice), 1981, 1982, 1985, 1988, 1989, 1990, 1991
Fourth edition 1995

Illustrations not otherwise credited prepared by Fraser Reekie

British Library Cataloging in Publication Data
A catalogue record for this book is available from the British Library

Library of Congress Cataloging-in-Publication Data
A catalog record for this book is available from the Library of Congress

ISBN 0 340 573244

1 2 3 4 5 95 96 97 98 99

Typeset in 10/11 pt Times by Anneset, Weston-super-Mare, Avon,
Printed in Great Britain by St. Edmundsbury Press Ltd, Bury St. Edmunds, Suffolk and
bound by J. W. Arrowsmith Ltd, Bristol

Contents

Preface to Fourth Edition

This new edition has been produced to satisfy the demand of students and lecturers, for whom the name Fraser Reekie is synonymous with good practice and sound advice. It is hoped that this edition will also appeal to a new generation of beginners who wish to learn how to communicate graphically through drawings, relating to design and construction.

In September 1992 HRH The Prince of Wales opened his Institute of Architecture, and from the outset the foundation course has stressed the importance of drawing as well as sketching 'out and about in London'. With this in mind it was decided that much of the original book be retained; new material and illustrations would only be added where necessary. It was decided, therefore, that the character of the book should not be changed.

This revised edition reinforces the importance of drawing by hand and continues the techniques and method pioneered by R. Fraser Reekie in the 1946 edition. Additionally, this edition takes into account recent developments in computer-aided design.

The third edition was published in 1976, and since then computeres have been introduced into drawing offices to give a range of graphic and modelling opportunities for designers to produce highly professional presentations in a relatively short time. This development was touched on in the third edition, (1976), and as was pointed out, CAD continues to be used in large firms and government agencies. However, today there are more small offices employing computer techniques.

Although it is desirable for students of planning, architecture, surveying and building construction to be aware of the terminology and the graphic possibilities of computers, this new edition is to remind the student of the book's purpose, which R. Fraser Reekie set out in the preface of the first edition: 'To describe the techniques and methods of preparing drawings used in connection with the lay-out, design and construction of buildings'.

These words were written in 1946 but are still relevant today. The basic principles of good drawing have not changed. Purpose, accuracy, legibility and neatness are essential elements whether the drawing is produced by computer or done 'freehand'. It is the purpose of this new edition to show that the traditional and conventional approach to drawing still has its place.

Tony McCarthy
1995

Fraser Reekie's Preface to Third Edition

A new edition of this book has been called for in order to make those changes which always become necessary from time to time as a result of developments in professional and industrial practice and, in this case, further teaching experience.

Since the preparation of the second edition seven years ago, there have been continued technological advances in the processes of design and construction. The overall effect has been to make evident a greater need than ever before for skills in relevant graphic techniques. The primary purpose of this book remains that of providing information and guidance with regard to these means of communication, for students in any way connected with planning, architecture, surveying and building.

In a general sense there is little I can add to what I wrote as prefaces to the first and second editions. These are reprinted in the following pages and they should be read in conjunction with these remarks. One of the changes that has taken place since the times in which they were written has been the proliferation of drafting aids, as can be seen in the now profusely illustrated catalogues of suppliers of drawing office materials. It is never possible to include all such equipment in a book or to give a picture of every latest item, but descriptions of basic types, of which it is helpful to have some knowledge, have been included. Future products for a long time to come are likely only to be variations.

Cognisance has also been taken of computer graphics. Although for reasons of cost and difficulties of availability their use up to the present has been confined mainly to large firms and government agencies, it is possible that with wider educational recognition of the capabilities of computers and with the expansion of computer services, there will be increased acceptance and utilisation in the future. It is desirable that there is an awareness of this trend.

The chapter on Freehand Drawing, formerly 'Freehand Sketches', has been re-written with added examples to give more emphasis to what manifestly has become of greater importance at all levels in all branches of technical and professional activities.

The opportunity has also been taken to rearrange sections of the book in a more logical order while including new and revised text material as required by the changes referred to above. A number of new illustrations have been added.

Production or working drawings, as in previous editions, have not been included in detail, not only because the limitations of page size make legible reproduction impossible, but also – a more important reason – because practice varies from country to country, from place to place and from office to office. It is intended that there should be an awareness of fundamentals, but it would be beyond the scope of this book, which is essentially concerned with graphic techniques rather than drawings *per se*, to attempt a comprehensive survey of such drawings. From various inquiries that have recently been made, it is interesting to find that the majority of working drawings are still being produced on traditional lines.

As the book is used internationally, references to the imperial system of measurement are retained.

In conclusion, I would like to say to those who are starting their studies that fluency in draughtsmanship is not merely a practical means of communication – sometimes the only adequate means – and of making and keeping records, but also a generator and refiner of ideas in the creative process and, not least, a continual source of pleasure to oneself and one's fellows.

Acknowledgements

I have no space to list with my grateful thanks the names of all the people in different parts of the world and at various times who have told me of their interest in the book and the many who have assisted me in the preparation of successive editions. It has been especially satisfying to learn that the book not only helped some when they were students but that it continued to be useful to them in their subsequent careers.

With regard to this edition, I would like to express particular thanks to the following, who gave of their time to discuss techniques and who provided new material: David G. Campion, Frank A. Evans, Graham Moss and Howard Tozer

I should like to thank the following who have given me sound advice and great assistance in the preparation of this update and who, in some cases, provided new photographs and drawings:

Henry Phillpotts; Paul Dyke; Barrie Christian; Maggie Black; David Eccles; Richard Trinnick; Anthony Blee; June Nicholas; Jacqueline Cullen; David Price; Eric Monk; Tim Monk; Malcolm M Read; Bob Steadman; The Society of Architectural and Industrial Illustrators; The graphics technicians in the Faculty of the built Environment of the University of the West of England.

MIDDLE

57

Gordon Cullen

This book is dedicated to the late Gordon Cullen

Thomas Gordon Cullen
CBE RDI Hon FRIBA(1914–1994)
was a Patron of the Society of Architectural
and Industrial Illustrators

Frontispiece: The art of urban design – the late Gordon Cullen's image of a proposed
vista in the Greenwich Peninsula, London, from Price & Cullen's competition
entry in 1988 ably shows how a drawing need not be laborious in order to
convey the designer's message powerfully.
*Fine-line fibre-tip pen, waxoil crayon and chinagraph
pencil on 112 gsm tracing paper, 210 × 290 mm.*

1
Drawing Equipment

The following notes deal with the principal items of drawing equipment required by the student and the draughter.

There are many different kinds of most of the articles mentioned. A full description of all would be tedious and is unnecessary. The aim here is to cover everything essential and to give guidance as regards general selection and use.

The beginner is advised to purchase the best available instruments that he or she can afford. While it is possible to make good drawings with very little or even improvised equipment when the occasion arises, it is foolish for the novice to acquire inadequate or inferior articles. It is also advisable to purchase drawing-office equipment and materials from reputable manufacturers and dealers.

In the UK many items are covered by British Standards Institution recommendations, e.g. drawing boards and T-squares BS 6381, setsquares BS 2459 and scales BS 1347, but these are primarily for the guidance of manufacturers and suppliers.

Drawing boards

Drawing boards are made in sizes to correspond with standard drawing paper sizes. The most suitable for general use are:

A1   920 mm × 650 mm
A0 1270 mm × 920 mm

which supersede the former standard sizes of: imperial (813 mm × 585 mm), and double elephant, (1067 mm × 813 mm). Boards of these old sizes and a larger size called antiquarian, (1372 mm × 813 mm) are still common and can be used for the appropriate smaller A sizes of paper. Various other sizes of board are made to suit draughting machines, which are referred to later in this chapter.

Fig. 1.1 illustrates two types of drawing board. Types A and B, not bigger than size A1, are suitable for the student as they are light for carrying about

DRAWING
BOARDS

BATTEN

A

B

Fig. 1.1

HEAD

Fig. 1.4

EBONY RULING EDGE

PERSPEX   "   "

FULL-SIZE SECTIONS THROUGH BLADES

BLADE

Fig. 1.2

T-SQUARE

Fig. 1.3

and are relatively inexpensive. Such boards can be obtained with metal edges.

It is important with all types of drawing board that the faces are perfectly flat and smooth, and that they will not twist or buckle with normal use. Edges should be at right-angles to one another. Wooden boards should have a firm even grain free from knots and should be soft enough to take drawing pins or staples easily and allow their removal without difficulty. Boards with composition surfaces can have paper attached by means of spring clips or strips of drafting tape as described later.

There are a number of desk top drawing units available now made from melamine board with parallel motion on metal stands and with a range of different working angles. Sizes A1 and A2. There is also a range of drawing stands with timber or metal folding legs. White plastic boards with parallel motion which can be adjusted for height and angle serve as either a drawing board or a layout table. The board dimensions vary, but 80 by 120 cm is usual for most drawing work (for further information see Drawing tables, page 21).

Care of drawing boards

The value of a good drawing board can only be maintained by careful treatment. The surface should be protected from knocks and scratches. If left on the table, the board should not be exposed to heat or moisture. Drawing pins should not be stuck in unnecessarily, and using the board as a backing on which to cut paper or card is harmful to the surface.

T-squares

T-squares or tee squares (Fig. 1.2) are described in shape by the name. They are used in conjunction with the board for drawing horizontal lines (Fig. 1.3), the head of the T-square being held against the left-hand side of the board by right-handed persons (reverse T-squares to operate against the right-hand side of the board are made for the left-handed draughter) .

Sizes correspond to the lengths of the drawing boards listed above:

A1 920 mm blade
A0 1270 mm blade

and for the old sizes: imperial, 32 in (812 mm); double elephant, 42 in (1066 mm); antiquarian, 54 in (1371 mm).

T-squares are best when made of mahogany with clear plastic ruling edges (Fig. 1.4).

In the UK the blade usually tapers, which makes the T-square more manageable when lifted by the head. In the USA and on the Continent of

Europe the blade is more often with parallel edges. They have necessarily to be made of thin strips of wood for lightness, but this renders them liable to fracture. They should therefore be handled with care and should not be left lying about in 'bridging', positions or leaning against walls. They should either be left flat or hung on pegs. Damage is also likely to arise in two other ways by careless handling: a loosening of the fixing between head and blade, and indentations along the ruling edge. Loose blades can often be tightened up with a screwdriver, but care must be taken to see that a true right angle is formed with the head. Blades that have become dented can be re-shot: a remedy that should not be attempted by the amateur. Most drawing equipment suppliers will carry out this and other repairs.

It is important to keep the underside of the blade smooth and clean, and this is best achieved by wiping it periodically with a soft cloth and a few drops of petrol or similar spirit. Water can be used, but is less effective and may cause warping. The underside is less likely to collect dust in traversing the paper if the tapered edge is rounded off, as shown in Fig. 1.4.

Set squares

A set square is used for drawing vertical and inclined lines. It is a triangle of clear plastic about 2 mm thick and adjustable, as illustrated in Fig. 1.5.

For general use, the length of the longest side should be about 230–300 mm and the edges should be square (Fig. 1.5), not bevelled. The square edge is less likely to cause smudging when ink lines are ruled.

A type of set square specially designed to prevent smudging is illustrated in Fig. 1.5B. It consists of the ordinary type of set square with additional thin strips stuck on both sides a short distance back from the edges, which are thus raised above the paper. A similar type has stepped edges.

As with T-squares, it is important to protect set squares from damage. Dents are caused by hard knocks, and cutting with a razor-blade etc. along the edges can easily ruin them. They should be kept scrupulously clean because dirty set squares quickly transfer the dirt to the drawing. For cleaning, soap and water is effective and does not harm plastic. Particular care should be paid to cleaning the edges of set squares.

Drawing instruments

Scales

Scales are thin narrow strips of white or yellow plastic, with divisions along each edge, usually on both sides. These divisions are in various recognized proportions to actual distances and dimensions, and can therefore be used

SQUARE EDGE

BEVELLED EDGE

SECTIONS *Fig. 1.5*

RAISED EDGE

B

STRIPS

ADJUSTABLE ARM

FIXING SCREW

SCALE OF DEGREES

HINGE

A

ADJUSTABLE SET-SQUARE

for making new drawings 'to scale' (see Chapter 5) or for measuring, by 'scaling', as it is termed, existing drawings.

Fig 1.6 shows the two sides of a scale for metric drawings. There are two lines of divisions along each edge in the proportions of 1:1 or 1:10/1:100, 1:20/1:200, 1:5/1:50, 1:250/1:2500. Other kinds of scale are available for land survey and town planning drawings.

Scales are usually 300 mm or 150 mm long. The longer is often more convenient in use, but the shorter can be carried in the breast pocket.

Scales are best if oval on section for architectural drawings so that the edges can be brought close to the surface of the paper for marking off or measuring distances. For surveying drawings the flat section is better. Scales should never be used for ruling lines or for any other purpose for which they are not intended; the edges are soon chipped and broken.

See Chapter 5 for descriptions of the scales used for various kinds of drawing.

Fig. 1.6 Metric scales. Illustration shows arrangement of scales on each side.

Protractors

A protractor (Fig. 1.7) is used for measuring or for setting out angles. It is a semicircular piece of metal or clear plastic with the arc divided into degrees' reading both to left and right, and with the centre and diameter indicated. The illustration shows how measurements are made. The protractor is placed so that the centre coincides with the apex of the angle and the diameter lies along one line, the position of the other line on the scale giving the reading.

The most convenient sizes have diameters from 100 mm to 150 mm. The transparent protractor is to be preferred' but, for architectural drawings' the instrument is superseded by the adjustable set square. They are, however, used in the plotting of surveys.

Curves

Fig. 1.8 illustrates a typical french curve. Made of clear plastic like set squares, they can be used for drawing irregular or complex curved lines that cannot be conveniently made up of arcs of circles. Many shapes are available, but one is usually sufficient for architectural drawing. They are not essential, and with practice curved lines can be drawn freehand more rapidly and often with better effect. Long, slow curves can be drawn by a series of blended straight lines with acceptable accuracy.

Another device is the flexible ruler consisting of a length of pliable plastic which can be bent to any required curve. Flexi curves made of a plastic outer cover and rubber flexible core, are also available for drawing curves. Patience is needed to get the correct curvature, but once set the ruler is particularly useful for repetition work.

Small circles and ellipses, or parts thereof, can often be more easily drawn with the help of plastic templates, which are available for figures of various metric and imperial sizes.

General comments

Chief amongst the personal equipment of the draughter is a set of instruments, and special attention should be taken in the selection and care of them. There is normally a wide range of kinds and patterns to choose from, and they can be bought separately or in sets. It is probably more economical to purchase the pieces individually in the beginning. Sets, in cases, usually contain one or more inessential items, and it is probably easier to test the instruments if they are bought singly. Cases are, of course, useful for keeping the instruments, which need to be protected when not in use. A suitable carrying-case can be made cheaply, however, by folding and sewing

RUBBER

PENCIL / INK

SOLVENT INK ERASER

Fig. 1.15

FRENCH
CURVE

Fig. 1.8

PENCIL

SCALE OF
DEGREES

50°   130°

DIAMETER   CENTRE

PROTRACTOR

Fig. 1.7

a piece of chamois leather to form a series of pockets. This can be rolled up and tied with tapes.

The most useful types of instrument described below are based on good typical examples.

All instruments should be carefully examined to see that they function properly. Needle points of compasses and dividers, drawing pens and pen compasses should be checked.

Dividers

Fig. 1.9 illustrates a pair of dividers used for dividing lines into equal units by trial and error and for multiplying or transferring distances. A convenient length is about 140 mm. A spring screw attachment to one leg for fine adjustment is an advantage. The hinge should move easily but should not be loose.

Compasses

Fig. 1.10 shows a common pattern of compasses, which are used for drawing circles and arcs. One leg terminates in a needle point and the other leg can be fitted with pencil or pen. An additional needle-pointed leg can also be obtained for converting this instrument into another pair of dividers for emergency use. For large circles and arcs a lengthening bar (Fig. 1.11) is valuable.

Both legs of the compasses are jointed so that they can be bent to keep the point more or less perpendicular to the paper.

Needle points are removable and are usually shouldered at one end. This end is best for use in drawing circles, as the point does not penetrate the paper too far. The instrument should be held at the top – see illustration of dividers in Fig. 1.9 – and pressure must be only sufficient to keep the centre from slipping and to maintain a smooth even line for the curve. The two points of the compasses must be carefully adjusted. The pencil lead should be the same grade as the ordinary pencil being used on the same drawing. A 12 mm length can be cut from the bottom of the pencil for the purpose. It should be sharpened to a fine chisel point and arranged tangential to the circumference, although for small circles a round point is probably better.

Pens are capable of adjustment in the manner of ruling pens described later. The thickness of the ink line should be tested at the side of the paper before the required curve is drawn. To avoid blots thick lines should be built up rather than drawn by opening the pen widely.

Uni-adaptors are available to accept most sizes of technical drawing pen, ballpoint pen, cutting knife, felt-tipped pen etc.

Beam compasses

For drawing larger circles than are possible with ordinary compasses and the lengthening bar, beam compasses, as illustrated in Fig. 1.12, can be used. They consist of a centre point and a fitting, with interchangeable pencil and pen legs, which are screwed to a bar to give the radius required.

Spring bows and pump compasses

Small dividers and pencil and pen compasses for accurate and fine work are called spring bows, and are illustrated in Fig. 1.13. Adjustment is made by means of a screw either at the side, as shown, or in the middle of the instrument. There are a number of variations of these instruments, including precision-made pump compasses and rapid adjustment compasses. It should be mentioned, however, that for general work small circles and arcs are drawn through templates (see p.15).

Drawing pens (sometimes called technical pens) ____

Straight lines in ink are ruled in conjunction with the T-square and set square by means of special drawing pens, such as the Rotring Rapidoliner, Rotring Isograph, or Staedtler drawing pens. These pens are based on the fountain-pen principle, with ink reservoirs so that they can be used for long periods without refilling. Interchangeable nibs or drawing elements are used for different thicknesses of lines, usually ranging from 0.2 mm to 1.2 mm; the consistency of line is a great advantage. The pens can also be used for the freehand drawing of lines and for. freehand and stencil lettering (see Chapter 4 for reference to guided pen lettering). The Graphos pen has special nibs for freehand lettering.

Instructions for use and care come with the pens, and it is only necessary here to emphasize how important it is to follow these instructions, which should be kept readily available for reference, especially in regard to cleaning. Much of the speed and convenience to be gained by using these pens can be lost if they are not properly looked after but are allowed to become clogged or encrusted with ink, so that undue time has to be wasted in making them work – with all the exasperation this can cause!

All kinds of drawing pen should be held perfectly upright against the edge of T-square or set-square, and should be drawn smoothly with even pressure from left to right or in an upwards direction. It may be found convenient to build up thick lines from two or three close rulings of thinner lines, but care must be taken at ends and corners that they do not become ragged.

Drawing ink

Waterproof black ink is used for line drawings. Cartridges can be filled straight from the bottle. There are also prefilled cartridges for use with the pens previously described.

Some inks are sticky and do not run freely; others are uneven in quality

Fig. 1.11

HORN CENTRE
FOR COMPASSES'
POINT

LENGTHENING BAR

INK LEG

SCREW FOR FINE ADJUSTMENT

JOINT

JOINT

PENCIL LEG

NEEDLE POINT

LEAD

DIVIDERS

COMPASSES

Fig. 1.9

Fig. 1.10

ADJUSTMENT SCREW

PEN LEG

PENCIL LEG

INK BOWS

DIVIDERS

PENCIL BOWS

SPRING BOWS *Fig. 1.13*

FIXING SCREW

BEAM

FIXING SCREW

NEEDLE POINT

PENCIL POINT (OR PEN)

Fig. 1.12

BEAM COMPASSES

DRAWING INSTRUMENTS

and deteriorate rapidly. A little experimenting will soon reveal the most satisfactory. Not all inks are suitable for the drawing pens described earlier in
this chapter or for use on all kinds of film, and the makers, recommendations should be followed.

Containers should always be kept closed, except when pens or instruments are being filled, to keep out dust and to lessen the risk of accidental
spills. A useful hint in avoiding the latter is to stand the bottle in a circular
hole in a block of wood or cardboard lid of a suitable size. Special iron and
rubber bottle-holders are sold for the same purpose. In warm weather it
may be found that the ink will run more freely if it is slightly diluted with
clean, preferably distilled, water. Bottles should not be shaken once they
are in use or any sediment that may have collected at the bottom will be disturbed. Inks should never be mixed and dirty pens must not be used: chemical action may be set up and the ink become lumpy.

Drawing inks are also obtainable in about twenty different colours.

Freehand pens

Every draughter requires some good freehand pens. Most manage very well
with two, one for very thin lines and the other for medium lines (Fig. 1.14).
Thick lines should always be built up. Most pens have to be worn in with
use, and then, when working well, become a valued possession.

Lettering pens and stencils

These are described later in Chapter 4

Pencils

Ordinary drawing pencils are made of cedarwood with 'leads' of compressed clay and graphite, and are about 175 mm long. The hexagonal type
is more easily held in the fingers, and the pencil does not roll off the board
or table. The value of a pencil is, generally, proportionate to its cost. The
best should always be used for drawing. It is false economy to buy cheap
pencils, the leads of which are gritty or crumbly and make good draughting
impossible.

Leads are made in varying degrees of hardness and softness, ranging from
9H, the hardest, to 6B, the softest. The extreme grades are very little used.
Most drawing can be carried out perfectly well in HB or F. Setting-out lines
and fine work may be done in H; rough sketching in B. Beginners, particularly, should not use pencils harder than H on cartridge and similar drawing

papers. It is a common error to resort to a hard pencil because the point lasts longer and the line is less likely to smudge; properly used, an HB pencil will keep its point just as long and will give a much better line while permitting greater freedom of wrist action. Hard pencils bite into the paper and make harsh wiry lines. Smudging is due to carelessness, and the student should learn to avoid rubbing the lines of his drawing. This matter has to be stressed' but no real progress in drawing can be made while hard pencils are used. References will be made later to the use of other types of pencil for particular purposes.

ERASER SHIELD

Fig. 1.18

INK ERASER

Fig. 1.17

FREEHAND PENS

Fig. 1.14

WATER JAR

SPONGE

WATER COLOUR DISHES

SAUCER

WASH BRUSH

Fig. 1.20

6 8 2

RED SABLE BRUSHES

Fig. 1.19

POSTER COLO

DESIGN COLO

COLOURS

Pencil points should be long, round, and evenly tapering, as shown in Fig. 1.15, page 8. The exposed lead should be about 10 mm long, and the wood cut back a further 10–15 mm. The point must be round, and then, if the pencil is slowly revolved as lines are drawn, it will wear away evenly and remain sharp for some time. So-called chisel points are useless except for compasses. Satisfactory lines cannot be drawn with blunt or jagged points.

Mechanical pencil sharpener, which can be screwed either to the table or wall. These are generally efficient and save a certain amount of labour, although the points usually need a final touch of the penknife. The small sharpeners that can be held in the fingers are much improved nowadays and are quite useful, although care must be taken that lead dust and shavings fall into a waste basket or are otherwise safely disposed of.

It must be realized that pencils require frequent sharpening when in continuous use, and the beginner should start with a good stock and not be surprized if they wear out quickly.

A popular alternative to the ordinary pencil is the clutch pencil of similar shape and size, consisting of a metal lead holder, into which 2 mm leads of varying degrees, usually from 4B to 6H, or various colours can be inserted (Fig. 1.16). A push button operates the clutch and enables the lead to be withdrawn or fully protected as required. The main advantage of the clutch pencil is that balance is always constant. A lead pointer is incorporated in the push button.

Erasers

Alterations, corrections, and the removal of unwanted pencil lines are best made by rubbing with a soft rubber or vinyl eraser. Erasers should be large enough to be easily gripped, but very large erasers last too long and, as the outside surface becomes hard and useless in time, it is probably better to keep to small sizes. When the surface of the eraser is affected it can be cut away or, if not too bad, rubbed clean on an odd scrap of paper: a procedure that is usually necessary if the eraser has not been used for some time.

For removing soft pencil shading, charcoal and pastel, which are smeared by an ordinary eraser, a special putty rubber must be used.

Ink lines on drawing paper are removed by hard erasers of shape shown in Fig. 1.17. As usually only a small portion of an ink drawing has to be removed and the surrounding lines disturbed as little as possible, the rubbing is best done through a thin metal or celluloid rubbing shield (Fig. 1.18) which has openings to suit areas to be erased. Ink lines on tracing paper are best removed by scraping gently backwards and forwards with a safety razor blade held vertically between finger and thumb.

Electrically operated erasers are sometimes installed in large drawing

TEMPLATES ELLIPSES and CIRCLES

clutch pencil

Fig. 1.16

offices. The machine, suspended over the drawing table, is drawn down to the surface of the paper, and a small motor rotates rapidly a piece of pencil rubber or ink eraser.

The small particles of rubber that result from rubbing out should be carefully removed from the surface of the paper by blowing or by lightly flicking with a clean, smooth duster. Some draughters can effectively remove the particles with sweeps of the palm of the hand. It is important, however the job is done, to remove every single crumb and, if the drawing is in pencil, not to smear the line.

A special ink eraser, which removes drawing inks from tracing paper and drafting film (but which cannot be used on paper) by chemical process is available. It has the advantage that clean new lines can be immediately drawn over the erased area.

Colours

Water-colours are extensively used for drawings of all types, from the conventional indication of materials on constructional drawings to full colour perspectives. For all purposes the colours are usually taken from tubes or pans; sticks and cakes are not often seen. Using colours from pans is thought to be more economical, but if left for any length of time the material becomes hard and is difficult to soften again quickly. Tube colours keep softer longer and are more quickly mixed and blended, but a certain amount is wasted every time they are used as it is impossible to calculate exactly how much to squeeze out. Tube colours keep cleaner; pans, especially if in a colour box, often get others colours mixed with them.

Further references are made to the use of water-colours later in this book, and some pigments are named. The beginner should purchase colours as required and so build up a working range gradually instead of starting out with an arbitrary selection, many of which may never be used. At the same time, only experience can reveal the possibilities of each, so a little exploration is to be encouraged.

A colour box is not a necessity and may be a nuisance; the colours can be kept quite well in any small box.

Artists' quality water-colours should always be used for work of any importance. Other qualities are more or less adulterated and good results cannot be obtained.

Poster colours

These, in small or medium-size pots and tubes, also play a large part in the colouring of many types of drawing. For similar purposes, but for better results, designers' quality gouache colours can be substituted. Further references are made later to technique.

Care and common sense will avoid the wasting and spoiling of colours. Caps should be replaced on tubes and jars promptly after use to prevent the contents becoming hard and unusable. Dirty brushes and dirty water should never be allowed to touch fresh colour. When mixing colours the brush must be rinsed clean before a new colour is taken up. The water jar should be large, with a wide mouth, and preferably of clear glass, so that it can be seen when the water gets muddy. The water should be changed when it becomes discoloured.

Dishes

Two or three large saucers and about half a dozen good-sized water-colour dishes, as sold in sets or nests, are required for mixing colours and holding washes. They should be glazed and white; coloured and patterned dishes affect the apparent hue of the pigments. Little jars or tins should not be used as heavy colours deposit particles of pigment at the bottom, which are not properly stirred up in the wash. Slopes and slant slabs are not much used as they do not hold a sufficient quantity of liquid for large drawings. Dishes should be thoroughly cleaned after use.

Brushes

Most requirements are met by three red sable brushes, sizes 2, 6, and 8, in metal ferrules and wood handles, (Fig. 1.19), and one camel-hair 'wash brush' in a quill (Fig. 1.20).

Brushes vary in quality and must be carefully selected. A poor brush can be a serious hindrance to success. Sable brushes should come to a fine point and should have plenty of spring in the hairs. The point of a brush can be tested by dipping it in water and drawing the hairs along the palm of the hand, turning it round at the same time. The hairs should come easily to a fine point: if not, the brush should be rejected. The 'spring' can be tested by gently pressing the hairs against the hand or other firm surface and feeling how they straighten again when the pressure is released. A brush without spring is of little value. The spring is soon destroyed, incidentally, by rough usage.

Wash brushes hold a good quantity of water, but do not come to a point, and for this reason some draughters prefer a large-size red sable' say No. 12.

Brushes must be kept clean. Colour should never be allowed to dry in the hairs. Brushes should be wiped carefully on a clean rag after washing and left standing upright in a jar' as illustrated in Fig. 1.19. They must not be left with the hairs in the water jar. If they have to be carried about they should be tightly held by a rubber band to a stiff strip of card somewhat longer than the longest brush or put in a plastic tube so that the hairs are protected.

Drawing papers

There are two main classifications of drawing papers: (1) machine-made papers, such as cartridge, which are used for exercises and line drawings, and (2) handmade or mouldmade papers used for rendered drawings. Mention is made of other types of paper, where necessary, in later chapters.

Cartridge

This is sold in rolls and A-size sheets, including pads of 30 sheets up to A2 size, as well as in the old standard sizes such as imperial. Fig. 1.21 shows A sheet sizes drawn to a comparative scale.

Paper is sold in different thicknesses. The rolls can be conveniently cut into the various standard sheets or used for extra large drawings' and are probably more economical for the busy office.

Unmounted cartridge paper has right and wrong sides, which can be distinguished by examination: the wrong side has a slightly but regularly pitted surface, and the cut edge of the sheet is usually turned down towards the wrong side.

The surface is fairly satisfactory for pencil drawing, and the heavy quality will take ink moderately well, but it is not really suitable for colour washes except those of a most limited nature.

Handmade and mouldmade papers

These are obtainable in sheets of standard sizes and usually in three surfaces: HP (Hot Pressed) – smooth; NOT – medium; R – rough. The first-named is the kind most used for pencil and ink drawings and various types of rendering, particularly work in wash. All the papers can be 'stretched' as described later in Chapter 10, and some can be obtained already mounted on stiff card or board. Water-colour paper is also sold in pads.

Plastic-coated card

For particularly fine pencil line and pen and ink drawings some draughters prefer an extremely smooth plastic-coated card. Great care is needed, however, in working with this medium as ink lines are easily smudged. Any

TRACING PAPER

SHORT ROLL OF
TRACING PAPER
FOR DESIGN STUDIES,
ETC.

Fig. 1.23

Fig. 1.21

dimensions in millimetres

DRAWING PAPER - STANDARD SIZES

punch
holes

a.

b.

c.

FOLDING FOR FILING A1

Fig. 1.22

removal of lines must be made by gently rubbing with a soft eraser, or by scratching carefully with a scalpel.

Sizes of drawing

The advantages of standardized sizes for drawings are that they enable a more economical use of drawing and tracing paper, sensitized paper for prints, etc., to be made, and that the binding together and storing of the drawings becomes easier.

Standardization is almost automatic when A sizes are used, and sheets of different size can be folded to a common size for filing in folders: for example A1 sheet, as illustrated by Fig. 1.22.

For folding for transmission by post or for loose storage drawings can be similarly folded. In all cases the title block appears uppermost for ready reference.

Tracing paper and film

These materials are specially treated paper, and polyester film of transparent or semi-transparent nature; when placed over an original drawing they allow the lines underneath to be clearly seen and so copied or traced. The tracings thus made can then be used as negatives for the making of any number of further copies by the photoprinting processes described in Chapter 8. Drawings can of course be made directly on the materials in question. Almost all production drawings are negatives of one kind or another.

Tracing paper is most economical if purchased in rolls, but for final drawings it is increasingly the practice in offices and in schools of architecture to use precut sheets in the A sizes (Fig. 1.23), often with printed border lines, title blocks, and sometimes modular or other grids, etc. and in two surfaces: smooth and rough. Different makes vary, however, so that it is difficult to particularize as to the most suitable; personal preference plays some part in selection. Thin papers are usually good enough for preliminary sketches but are too flimsy for final negatives. Smooth surfaces are best for pencil drawings, as the rough kinds wear down the leads and tend to smudge and smear.

Detail paper

This paper, which is supplied in rolls and pads of 100 sheets (called layout pads) up to A2 size, is like thick tracing paper and is used chiefly for preliminary sketch drawings and layouts, and for final large-scale details. It is transparent enough for copying by tracing yet is white enough for original work to show up clearly, and it takes coloured pencils or felt and fibre pens satisfactorily. Acceptable dye-line prints can usually be obtained, especially from ink or strong pencil lines. Detail paper is also commonly used for computer graphic output.

Backing sheets

Wooden drawing boards should be covered with backing sheets, over which the actual drawing paper. or tracing medium is placed to provide a firm, even working surface. This is particularly important if boards have become pitted, scored, damaged or worn.

Thick white cartridge paper is a satisfactory material, cheap enough to be discarded as it becomes soiled; drawing pins can be used.

In connection with backing sheets, a useful device to minimize the marking of drawings by rubbing of the T-square is the fixing of a strip of folded drawing or tracing paper – three or four thicknesses are sufficient – about 20 mm wide along the left-hand edge of the board. Fixing at the ends only is best.

Drawing boards with an integral plastic surface do not normally require backing sheets, but for working on tracing paper a white undersheet is an advantage.

Fixings

The way of holding the paper to the board is to use drafting tape or Scotch tape. Drafting tape tends to be an untidy and rather messy fixing method except for short-term use. For holding one piece of tracing paper over another, especially where the piece is relatively small, transparent self-adhesive tape, such as Sellotape, is most suitable as it can be peeled away on completion without affecting the paper.

Drawing tables

It is beyond the scope of this book to deal in detail with major items of drawing office equipment: for this information, reference can be made to the appropriate British Standard Institution publications, and to manufacturers' catalogues.

However, the two most common working arrangements are: the drawing table, about 920 mm high, with level top on which the drawing board is placed, usually tilted slightly by means of a block or tapered subframe, and used in conjunction with a T-square and set-squares; or one of the various types of drawing board mounted on a stand or secured at the front of a table and, although capable of adjustment, used in an almost upright position in combination with a parallel motion sliding horizontal rule and/or drafting machine (Fig. 1.24).

The first arrangement has the merits of simplicity, economy, adaptability and mobility – it is little trouble to transport the ordinary board and T-square – which are certainly advantageous for the student. Drawings have to be made standing or sitting on a high stool, which many people prefer for freedom of movement, but a real disadvantage of the arrangement is that as the board cannot be tilted more than 15° without the T-square and set-squares slipping down, there is often difficulty in working comfortably at the top of larger boards. Although there are ways of mitigating this problem, the second arrangement does overcome it and also enables the draughter, if he or she so wishes, to work sitting in a swivel chair (Fig. 1.25). This arrangement, provided the board is kept upright, is also more economical in floor space; but it is virtually a fixed arrangement more suited to the office than the studio.

In all cases there should be nearby horizontal surfaces for the laying out of reference drawings and other papers and for placing instruments, together with drawers and cupboards for storage.

Minor items of equipment

In addition to the essential equipment already described, the following should be readily available for use as the need arises:

- A good pair of scissors. Cutting knives, e.g. a Stanley knife for thick card and a lighter knife, of which there are many kinds, for thin card and paper. In this connection' a metal rule or straight-edge is useful.
- A magnifying glass for examining small-scale maps and drawings and for executing fine draughting.
- Rolls of drafting tape – sometimes referred to as masking tape are useful. Arrowmounts, obtainable from photographic shops; these are small adhesive squares for the invisible mounting of photographs, but they are also useful for mounting drawings on paper (unless very flimsy) and thin card without the risk of cockling or distortion that the application of gums or pastes might cause. However, conventional gums and pastes are needed, and aerosol spray adhesives for heavier or other appropriate purposes.
- A supply of preprinted gridded paper, i.e. divided into squares of 2 mm or larger, for use under sheets in freehand approximate scale drawings on tracing or detail paper. Pads of tracing paper with fold-under grids are useful in many situations.

Fig 1.24   A drawing board being used in conjunction with a parralel motion sliding horizontal rule.

- A handy scratch pad for notes, memos, rough calculations, testing pens, etc.
- A clean duster.
- For the safe-keeping or transporting of personal drawings a good portfolio, while not a necessity, is desirable. The simplest kind can be made from two equal rectangular pieces of stout cardboard of adequate size loosely connected down one pair of long sides and provided with tapes at intervals along the other edges for tying together. They can, however, be purchased ready made, as can more elaborate flexible zip-around portfolios. The latter are only suitable for mounted drawings. Plastic and cardboard stoppered tubes of various sizes can be used for mailing or carrying rolled drawings.
- The use of aerosol fixers, lacquers and adhesives can create unpleasant fumes and odours. There are now three-stage fibre filters for the removal of spray particles and any harmful hydrocarbons. These fume cupboards are essential for draughters who wish to work in a clean solvent free environment.

MOVABLE WORK PLACE

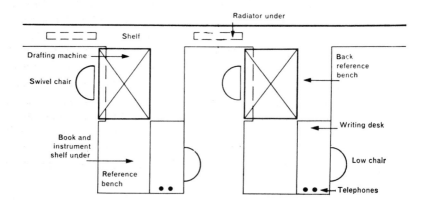

FIXED WORK PLACE

Fig.1.25 Examples of drawing-table arrangements. (Reproduced by permission from the RIBA Handbook of Architectural Practice and management, Part 2.670: Equipment of Drawing Offices)

2
Line Drawing

Pencil drawing

Almost everyone has 'drawn' with a pencil from an early age, but little benefit is usually derived from this kind of intermittent and undirected practice. Only bad habits seem to be formed. It is wise, therefore, on setting out to make a serious study of draughting, to forget any previous ideas of drawing, and to start as if pencil and paper had never been handled before.

In the previous chapter something was said about the materials required and the use of various instruments. Preliminary exercises in pencil drawing can be carried out with the aid of drawing board, T-square and set squares, H and HB pencils, and good-quality cartridge paper.

The first step is to learn how to draw straight lines. Straight lines in pencil should be *firm, clean,* and of *even strength*. Start by fixing down the paper, right side up, squarely on the board. Sharpen an HB pencil, as previously described. Give the T-square a wipe with a duster and place it on the board with the head against the left-hand edge. If you are left-handed you can get a special T-square that can be held against the right-hand edge of the board, but most left-handed draughters seem to manage quite well in the ordinary way. Holding the T-square steady in a position towards the top of the sheet, draw with the pencil along the ruling edge from left to right, pressing the point on the paper sufficiently to make a clear line, but not so hard as to make a groove. Turn the pencil slowly round in the fingers as you move it along. The completed line should be exactly the same thickness and strength throughout its length. Make sure that the pencil keeps the same angle with the T-square from start to finish or the line will be wavy.

Now move the T-square down the paper and repeat the operation. If necessary, try to improve on the first line. Draw a number of parallel lines in this way until you are satisfied with the quality of the lines. If you find the line becoming 'woolly' Fig. 2.1, it is probably because the pencil needs sharpening. If the line is uneven and broken, it may be that your arm or wrist movement is jerky and the pressure erratic; to correct this is merely a matter of muscular control, which comes with practice.

Having drawn a few good horizontal lines, pass on to the use of set squares and the drawing of vertical and inclined lines. Take the closed adjustable set square and with it, practise drawing lines with it, as shown in

I. HORIZONTAL   2. VERTICAL AND 45°

3. PARALLEL   *TO ANY GIVEN LINE*

LINES SHOULD BE FIRM, CLEAN, AND OF EVEN QUALITY

NOT COARSE AND 'WOOLLY'

NOR DOUBLE AND BROKEN

STRAIGHT LINES   *Fig. 2.1*

Fig. 2.1 (2). One edge of the set square rests on the blade of the T-square and is held in position where required by the left hand, which also holds the T-square firm. Lines are drawn with the pencil along the other edges of the set square in the directions indicated by the arrows. A number of parallel lines should be drawn bearing in mind the precautions mentioned above.

The adjustable set square set to a 60° angle can be used for vertical lines and for lines at 60° and 30° to the horizontal.

When a number of lines are to be drawn parallel to an inclined line, as may occur in the setting out of roof tiling, etc., the method shown in Fig. 2.1 (3) can be used. Place a set square along the inclined line so that another of its edges is at right-angles to the line. Then gently bring up the T-square until it is against this edge of the set square and hold it tightly, then, by moving the set square along the T-square to the required positions, lines parallel to the first one can be drawn. This method should be practised with lines at varying angles.

Remember in all cases to keep the pencil well sharpened and held properly against the ruling edge.

The second step in learning to use the pencil is to combine lines so as to construct figures and shapes, e.g. squares, rectangles, etc. Fig. 2.2 (1, 2 and 3) shows the setting up of a rectangle. Two parallel horizontal lines are first drawn any suitable distance apart, say, 50–60 mm. The lines should be faint though clear and regular. Their exact length is not important. On the lower line two points, A and B, are marked (in the example the distance between A and B is made the same as the distance between the lines, so the resulting figure is a square). Using the set square, two vertical lines are now drawn through A and B to cross the first two lines. These also are faint lines and are termed *construction lines*, and to bring out the required figure they have to be strengthened where necessary. This is shown in Fig. 2.2 (3) by a thickening of those parts of the lines that actually define the rectangle, but in a pencil drawing the lines need not necessarily be made thicker as long as they are made stronger, i.e. 'blacker', by going over the faint lines and putting more pressure on the pencil. Care must be taken that the 'lining in' as it is sometimes called is done exactly over the construction lines and that irregular or double lines do not result.

Note that the final lines do not cross where they meet at the corners of the rectangle. This gives added definition to the shape and gives a sharper, cleaner appearance to the drawing. It is a widely adopted custom in architectural drawing.

Fig. 2.2 (4) shows the crossing of lines at a junction to a larger size, and also a bad example where the lines fail to meet.

Fig. 2.2 (5) shows the making of a junction of three lines.

Fig. 2.2 (6) shows the right-angle junctions of several pairs of lines.

Lines can be made a little stronger by putting more pressure on the pencil. Such a slight emphasis to the ends of final lines can quickly become an unconscious habit with practice, and the effect is to increase greatly the legibility and attractiveness of the drawings.

In drawing circles and arcs the positions of the centres should be established first and the principal axes, i.e. horizontal and vertical lines passing through the centres, should be lightly drawn. Along one of these lines the length of the radius in each case can be marked and the curve drawn with compasses; see Fig. 2.2 (7).

If arcs are to be joined to straight lines, it is always better to draw the curves first. In the case of an example such as Fig. 2.2 (8 and 9), the axes should be drawn lightly first, then the arc with compasses also lightly, and then the vertical lines from the points where the arc cuts the horizontal axis. The strengthening of the lines should be done in the same order: i.e. the arc, or semicircle as it is, first, and then the vertical lines.

When the above elementary steps in architectural drawing have been mastered, a sound basis has been laid for the making of any drawing in line.

CONSTRUCTION LINES

FINAL LINES

A   B
1.

A   B
2.

A   B
3.

4.   5.   6.

HORIZONTAL AXIS

VERTICAL AXIS

7.

STRAIGHT LINES
AND ARCS
Fig. 2.2   8.   9.

SMOOTH
CONTINUOUS LINE
PENCIL HELD WELL
BACK FROM POINT

JERKY,
BROKEN AND
WOOLLY LINE

CURVED LINE
THROUGH
PLOTTED
POINTS

FREEHAND
CIRCLE

FREEHAND   CURVES   *Fig. 2.3*

A word might be said here on freehand drawing, although this is dealt with further in a later chapter, as a certain amount comes into almost every drawing. The main principle is to get the same quality and strength in the freehand lines as in those drawn with instruments. The tendency to be guarded against is the coarsening of the freehand lines. It is a matter of practice, but keep the pencil well sharpened and try to draw smooth, *continuous* freehand lines with even pressure. Avoid 'sketchy' lines made with jerky movements. Hold the pencil well back from the point for long, flowing curves. Sometimes, when the curve is long and sinuous, it is easier to draw if a number of points along its length are first lightly plotted. Small freehand circles can be best drawn as two curves, as indicated by the arrows in Fig. 2.3.

Keeping the drawing clean

It is important to keep drawings as clean as possible and to preserve the surface of the paper, especially if colour is to be used. To these ends the following points should be constantly kept in mind.

- Use clean equipment and instruments and good pencils.
- Keep hands clean and touch the paper with the fingers as little as possible.
- Avoid unnecessary rubbing of the surface of the paper with T-squares and set squares. Move them by lifting rather than by sliding. A piece of paper folded two or three times to make a narrow strip about 25 mm wide and pinned along the left-hand side of the board is helpful in lifting the T-square blade just clear of the paper and so reducing friction.
- Sharpen pencils away from the drawing board and table.
- Make any erasures carefully and remove all crumbs by blowing or lightly flicking with clean handkerchief or hand.
- If much drawing is to be done on several small areas of the sheet, cover the whole of it with tracing or detail paper in which suitable flap 'windows' through which to work can be cut.

Inking-in

If a drawing is to be finished in ink, it is always better to draw it first completely in pencil, taking just as much care as if it were to be so finished. The inking then becomes a straightforward process without innumerable breaks for the working out of details and the correcting of mistakes, and time is thereby probably saved in the long run. There is no excuse for making a careless, dirty pencil drawing on the grounds that it is subsequently to be inked in.

The methods of using drawing pens and other instruments have already been described. The sequence in inking in should generally be as follows:

1. Centre lines.
2. Circles and arcs, drawn with ink compasses.
3. Horizontal lines.
4. Vertical and inclined lines.
5. Hatching and blacking-in of sectional parts, etc.
6. Dimensions lines.
7. Freehand lines, arrows and arrowheads. dimension figures, notes.
8. Titles, etc.

To avoid being held up while some lines are drying, it may not be possible to keep strictly to this sequence, but systematic working reduces the chances of errors and omissions. As with pencil drawing, main outlines should be strengthened for increased definition and meeting lines should slightly cross in architectural drawings.

If erasures are necessary, an ink eraser (page 3) can be used *gently* until the lines or blots are removed. For small areas or short lines a sharp razorblade held vertically to the surface of the paper and moved quickly backwards and forwards do the job. The surface must not be roughened, or subsequent ink lines will run and become ragged, although this tendency can be overcome to some extent by smoothing the affected area by pressure from a hard, rounded object such as a table-knife handle.

When the inking has been completed and checked, a soft pencil eraser should be used over the sheet to remove any dirt and pencil lines.

Geometrical drawing

Having acquired the elementary technique of line drawing, the next requirement is practice and yet more practice. Geometrical drawing is an excellent way of obtaining this practice and at the same time a knowledge of various constructions and figures continually used in the making of technical drawings.

Division of lines

Fig. 2.4 shows a number of ways of dividing straight lines into equal parts.

The first is by trial and error, using dividers. This is a fairly quick way, and with practice the required distances can be estimated very closely the first time. Spring-bow dividers are used for very short lines to be divided with great accuracy. If the line is comparatively long and the divisions numerous, it is sometimes easier to do the dividing in two stages. For example, if 20 divisions are required, the line might first be divided into four equal parts and each of these parts into five. Be careful to avoid pressing the divider points into the paper: mark off the required divisions with a touch of the pencil.

Fig. 2.4 (2) shows a graphical method of dividing a line into any number of equal parts. From one end of the line to be divided, AB in the example, another light line is drawn at an acute angle and along it are plotted equal units of any convenient length. From the end of the last of these units, marked 5, a light line is then drawn to B, and parallel lines are drawn from the intermediate points, thus dividing AB into a similar number of equal parts. This principle is a useful one to remember, and can often be employed using a scale or rule, as shown in (5), to divide into any number of equal parts the distance between two parallel lines. It is, for example, a speedy way of setting out the steps of a staircase.

To bisect a line – that is, to divide it into two equal parts – one method is to use compasses, as shown in (3), but for horizontal or vertical lines it is quicker to use a set square, as shown in (4). By the former method the ends of the line A and B are taken as centres for the two similar arcs of any radius greater than half AB; a line drawn through the intersections of the arcs on either side of AB cuts AB exactly in the middle. Using a set square, preferably 45°, lines at the same angle are drawn from the ends of line AB to intersect. A perpendicular from the intersection to the line bisects it. From this, further similar constructions can be made to divide the line into 4, 8, 16 parts, and so on, although it is unsuitable for more than eight. This latter method is useful for the finding of centre-lines, etc.

Plane geometry

It is assumed in the following descriptions of the setting up and drawing of common examples of plane figures that it is understood how the lines are drawn using T-square, set squares, etc.

Squares

The simplest way to draw a square, the sides of which are horizontal and vertical on the sheet, is shown in Fig. 2.5 (1). A horizontal line is drawn and the given or known length of one side of the square is marked on it (marked AB in the example). From A a light line is drawn at 45° to cut a perpendicular from B; from A another perpendicular is drawn and to it a horizontal line is drawn from the intersection of the 45° line and the perpendicular from B. i.e. C. ABCD is the required square.

Alternatively, Fig. 2.5 (3), the square could be drawn with the aid of compasses or dividers. Having drawn side AB and erected a perpendicular from

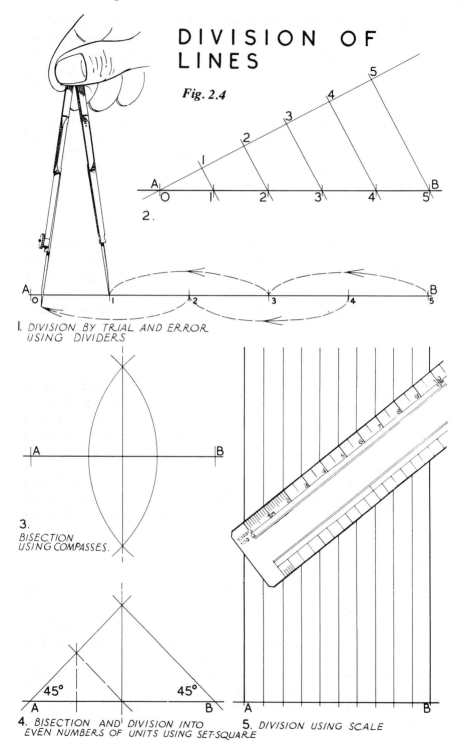

DIVISION OF LINES

Fig. 2.4

2.

I. DIVISION BY TRIAL AND ERROR USING DIVIDERS

3. BISECTION USING COMPASSES.

4. BISECTION AND DIVISION INTO EVEN NUMBERS OF UNITS USING SET-SQUARE

45°   45°

5. DIVISION USING SCALE

A, with centre A and radius AB an arc is drawn to cut the perpendicular at D. A horizontal line through D and a perpendicular from B complete the figure. There is, of course, no need to draw a complete arc from B to D; it is sufficient if the arc merely cuts the perpendicular from A. Similarly, AD could be set off by dividers or, in some case, marked off from a scale, although this often leads to inaccuracy.

Fig. 2.5 (2) shows a square with sides at 45 ° to the horizontal and vertical. This could be drawn by first drawing side AC, then a horizontal from A and a 45° line from C to cut it at B. and then 45° lines from A and B to meet at D. A line joining C and D is vertical and, incidentally, the intersection of the two diagonals is the centre of the square.

Rectangles

A rectangle is a four-sided figure with equal opposite sides and its angles all right angles. Assuming the lengths of its sides are known, one side is first drawn, AB in Fig. 2.6 (1), and perpendiculars are erected from A and B. Along one of these the length of the adjoining side AD is set off, and the figure is completed by drawing a line from D parallel to AB, cutting the perpendicular from B at C.

Rhomboid

Of other parallelograms, the setting up of which is similar, the rhomboid is shown in Fig. 2.6 (2). The rhomboid is a figure having equal opposite sides, but no right angles. The lengths of the sides and angles must be known before the drawing can be made, but if one angle is known the others can be calculated. One side, AB say, is drawn and from A at the known angle AD is set off equal to the length of the adjoining side. From D a line is drawn parallel to AB, and from B a line parallel to AD; the intersection of these lines at C gives the required figure, ADCB. A perpendicular to AB from D gives a line DE along which the distance between sides AB and DC can be measured.

Triangles

An equilateral triangle (three equal sides and three equal angles, each 60°), is very simply set up by drawing one side and from each end drawing lines at 60° to intersect, Fig. 2.7 (1). Alternatively, having drawn one side AB, arcs with centres at A and B and radius equal to AB can be drawn to intersect at C. Joining A and B to C by straight lines completes the figure.

An isosceles triangle (two equal sides and two equal angles) can be similarly constructed by drawing first the unequal side and from each end of it drawing lines at the known equal angles to intersect, Fig. 2.7 (2), or, alternatively, having drawn one side AB, with centres A and B and radius equal

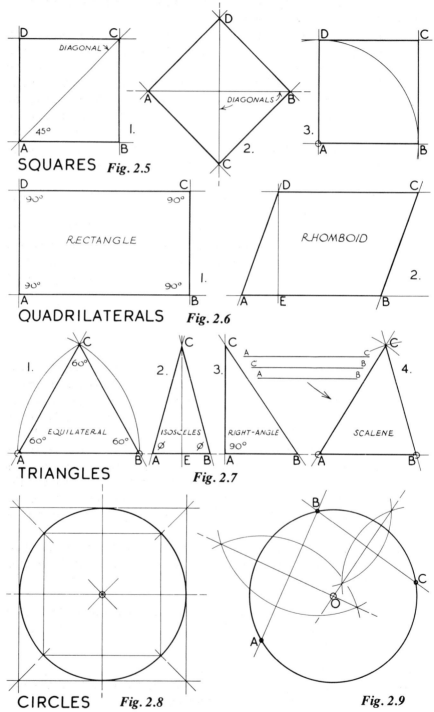

SQUARES *Fig. 2.5*

QUADRILATERALS   *Fig. 2.6*

TRIANGLES   *Fig. 2.7*

CIRCLES   *Fig. 2.8*

Fig. 2.9

to the equal sides drawing arcs to intersect at C. Joining A and B to C by straight lines completes the figure.

A right-angled triangle (having two sides at right angles to each other) can be set up by drawing one side adjacent to the right angle, erecting a perpendicular of required length at one end and by joining the two free ends. This method applies if the lengths of the two sides at right angles are known. If only one of these sides and the third side is known, the method is to draw the known side adjacent to the right angle; at one end of it to erect a perpendicular and then with the other end as centre and with radius equal to the other known side to draw an arc to cut the perpendicular. A line drawn from the intersection to the centre of the arc completes the figure.

To draw a scalene triangle (one having three unequal sides and unequal angles), the lengths of the sides being known, the method – which is applicable to any triangle and is particularly useful when no side is horizontal or vertical on the sheet – is shown in Fig. 2.7 (4). Any side AB is drawn and then with A and B as centres and with radii equal to the lengths of the other two sides, arcs are drawn to intersect at C. Joining A and B to C by straight lines completes the figure.

Circles

Reference has already been made to the drawing of circles and the advisability of establishing centres by lightly drawing the horizontal and vertical axes. Fig. 2.8 shows how circles can be drawn around and within squares. In the first case, the middle of the square is found by drawing its diagonals; with this point as centre and with radius equal to half the length of a diagonal a circle can be drawn to pass through the corners of the square. In the second case, the middle of the square is found as before, but the radius is made equal to half the length of one side: that is, the pencil point of the compasses is made to pass through the intersections of the axes and the sides of the square. It is obvious from the foregoing how squares can be drawn within or outside circles.

Fig. 2.9 shows the plotting of a centre of a circle that is required to pass through the points A, B. and C. AB and BC are both bisected by the method described in Fig. 2.4 (3). The point O. the intersection of the bisectors, is the centre of the circle.

Fig. 2.10 illustrates various terms descriptive of parts of circles and of lines in relation to circles. Brief definitions, in addition to those previously mentioned, are:

Arc	A part of the circumference.
Chord	A straight line. shorter than the diameter, terminated by the circumference at both ends.

Circumference	A curve line equidistant from a point, the *centre*, confining the circle.
Diameter	A straight line passing through the centre of the circle and terminated at both ends by the circumference.
Normal	A straight line drawn from any point on the circumference in a direction radial to the centre of the circle.
Quadrant	A quarter of a circle in shape and area.
Radius	A straight line drawn from the centre of a circle to the circumference. (plural *radii*).
Radial	A line in the direction of a radius, e.g. the joint lines of a masonry arch.
Sector	A part of a circle.
Segment	A part of a circle contained between a chord and its arc.
Semicircle	A half-circle in shape and area; the part on either side of a diameter.
Tangent	A straight line touching the circumference of a circle at one point at right angles to a normal at that point. In drawing a tangent to an arc, it is better to draw a radius to the tangential point first and then to draw the tangent at right angles to it, rather than to judge the meeting of the straight line and curve by eye. See Fig. 2.4.

In Fig. 2.11 (1, 2, 3, 4, 7 and 8) are examples of combinations of arcs, and of arcs and straight lines. The construction lines are shown and the centres indicated so that the setting up can be followed and similar exercises practised. The important point to observe is the part played by the construction lines in making easier the accurate joining of the lines.

Fig. 2.11 (5) shows the junction of a quadrant arc with two lines at right angles. This is often done by trial and error with unsatisfactory results. The correct method is to draw a light line at 45° from the intersection of the two straight lines and another parallel to one of them and away from it a distance equal to the radius of the required arc. The meeting of this line with the 45° line gives the centre for the curve. If, however, the size of the arc is to be judged by eye, the 45° line will be helpful in locating the centre of it.

When the arc is to connect two straight lines not at right angles, as in Fig. 2.11 (6), the method is to draw lines parallel to each of the straight lines at distance away from them equal to the radius of the required arc. The point of intersection is the centre of the arc.

Ellipse

The ellipse comes frequently into architectural drawing, not only as a curve or shape in itself, but also in the representation of circles in various projections, etc. There are several methods of setting up the figure; some locate points on the curve, which has to be completed freehand; others give cen-

NORMAL

90° 90°

90°

TANGENT

CIRCUMFERENCE

D

RADIUS

RADIALS

SECTOR

QUADRANT

A

DIAMETER

HORIZONTAL AXIS

B

VERTICAL AXIS

CHORD

SEGMENT

ARC

Fig. 2.10

C

1.

2.

3.

4.

EQUAL TO RADIUS

5.

EQUAL TO RADIUS

EQUAL TO RADIUS

6.

Fig. 2.11

7.

8.

CIRCLE & ARCS

tres from which curves approximating to an ellipse can be drawn. Fig. 2.12 (1 and 2) are examples of the former; Fig. 2.12 (3 and 4) of the latter.

1. The ellipse is constructed in a lightly drawn rectangle, EFGH, with sides equal to the major and minor axes, AB and CO. The half major axis AO is divided into a number of equal parts, three in the example (the number depends on the size of the drawing, but as few as possible is advised), and EA is also divided equally into a similar number of parts. Lines are then drawn from C through the divisions on AO to intersect corresponding lines drawn from O to the divisions on EA. The curve of a quarter of the ellipse has now to be drawn carefully and smoothly through the points of intersection. The rest of the ellipse can be completed by repeating the construction or by plotting or transferred tracing from the curve already drawn.

2. The trammel method is preferred by most draughters as it avoids the numerous construction lines of the foregoing and other methods. The major and minor axes are first drawn, AB and DC, intersecting at O. A straight strip of card or stout paper (the trammel) is then taken, placed with its edge along the major axis and, with a pencil, half the length of the axis, e.g. OB, is marked on it. The trammel is then placed with its edge along the minor axis so that half the axis, OD, can be marked on it within and from one end of the previous marking. By placing the trammel on the drawing so that the two marks separated by the difference between the two axes on the axes as shown, and then moving the trammel but always keeping those marks on the axes, the third mark can be made to trace the curve of the ellipse, and a series of light pencil dots gives the plotting.

   The construction of ellipses in the ways described above is only satisfactory where the required sizes are sufficiently large for reasonably accurate setting out. For small curves, unless one's freehand is particulary good, it is easier and better to draw through plastic guides or templates, which are obtainable for various sizes and proportions.

3. The construction of half of a pseudo-ellipse formed of arcs struck from three centres is illustrated in Fig. 2.12 (3). AB is the major axis and AO, less than half AB, is the estimated radius of the first part of the curve, O being the centre for the arc, which is continued to cut the minor axis at E. DE is then bisected and the bisector is continued to cut the line of the minor axis at O, which is the centre for the arc FG (radius OE drawn through D). HB is equal to AD.

4. The construction of half a pseudo-ellipse formed of arcs struck from five centres is shown in Fig. 2.12 (4). AB is the major axis and OC is half the minor axis. A rectangle AFEB is first set up on AB, the sides AF and EB being equal to OC. A line is drawn from AC and at right angles to it a line FG is drawn cutting AB at H. H is the centre for the first part of the curve. Then, with centre O and radius OC an arc is drawn to cut AB at J.

With JB as diameter a semicircle is drawn, from the centre of which a perpendicular is erected to cut the semicircle at L. Along CG from O a distance OM equal to KL, the vertical from EF to the curve of the semicircle is marked, and with centre G and radius GM an arc is drawn to cut arcs struck from centres A and B with radius equal to ON, see drawing. The centres for the curves are G, H, P, Q and R.

There are other settings out of pseudo-ellipses. They are much used for brick and masonry arches. Careful drawing is essential, the construction lines being made as light as possible.

Parabola

Parabolic lines and shapes are often required to be drawn, and the simplest setting up for most general purposes when the required 'height' and 'width' are known is shown in Fig. 2.13. AB is the 'width' or baseline and CD the 'height' or axis. The rectangle AEFB is constructed; AE and FB are then divided into a number of equal parts, and AC and CB are similarly divided. Lines are drawn from D to the points of division on AE and on FB to cut corresponding perpendiculars drawn from the points of division on AC and CB. A smooth curve carefully drawn through the points of intersection is the required parabola.

Regular polygons

A brief description is given below of the setting-up of the pentagon (five equal sides), the hexagon (six equal sides), and the octagon (eight equal sides), as these are the polygons most commonly required in drawing.

Pentagon

Fig. 2.14 (1). If it is required to draw a pentagon within a known circle, the simplest practical method is to divide the circumference of the circle into five equal parts using dividers, and then to join the points with straight lines (Fig. 2.14 (1)). This method can, of course, be used for any regular polygon. If the base of the pentagon is to be horizontal, then the divisions should start from the top of the circle, i.e. where the vertical axis cuts the circumference.

If the length of the sides is known, the old but accurate method also shown in Fig. 2.14 (1) can be used. One side is drawn horizontally and with centres a each end of it and radius equal to its length arcs are drawn to intersect. Through the intersection a vertical line is drawn. One of the arcs, from the point of intersection to the horizontal line is divided into six equal parts. With the point of intersection as centre and radius equal to the chord of the

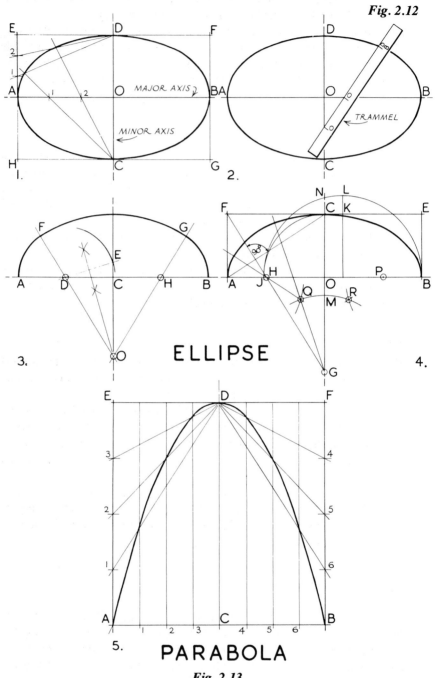

Fig. 2.12

ELLIPSE

PARABOLA

Fig. 2.13

first division an arc is drawn to cut the vertical line. The point so obtained is the centre of a circle that will contain the required pentagon.

If it is required to draw a pentagon about a given circle, the easiest way is to divide up the circumference into five equal parts, draw radii to the points so obtained, and then tangents to the same points. The tangents form the pentagon, (Fig. 2.14 (4)). This method can again be used for any regular polygon. The radii are drawn to facilitate drawing the tangents.

Hexagon

Within a circle a hexagon can be imply drawn by drawing a horizontal and lines in both directions at 60° through the centre to cut the circumference, and then by joining the points so obtained by straight lines, which are also horizontal or at 60°. Or, the radius of the circle can be stepped off around the circumference: it goes exactly six times (Fig. 2.14 (2).

If the length of each side of the figure is known, its construction using the 60° set square is obvious from the example.

To draw the figure around a circle, again a horizontal and lines at 60° are drawn through the centre to the circumference and tangent lines are drawn through the points of contact (Fig. 2.14 (5).

Octagon

Within a circle an octagon can be constructed by drawing the horizontal and vertical axes and lines at 45° to the circumference, and then by joining the points so obtained by straight lines, Fig. 2.14 (3).

If the length of each side of the figure is known, it is simplest to draw one side horizontally and then, with an adjustable set square, to draw lines at $67\frac{1}{2}°$ from each end of it to meet at a point that is the centre of the octagon. This enables a circle to be drawn, along the circumference of which can be set out the necessary distances or points for the completion of the figure.

To draw an octagon about a circle, the horizontal and vertical axes and lines at 45° in both directions through the centre are drawn to find tangential points on the circumference. The tangents can then be easily drawn with T-square and 45° set square.

Irregular quadrilaterals

Two examples of these figures are illustrated in Fig. 2.15. In the first, the 'kite' shape can be set up by drawing the diagonals first and measuring the required distances along them from the point of intersection. In the second example, which is likely to be a matter of copying or plotting a survey, the lengths of the sides would have to be known and also either the angles between them or the lengths of the diagonals. If the angles are known, then

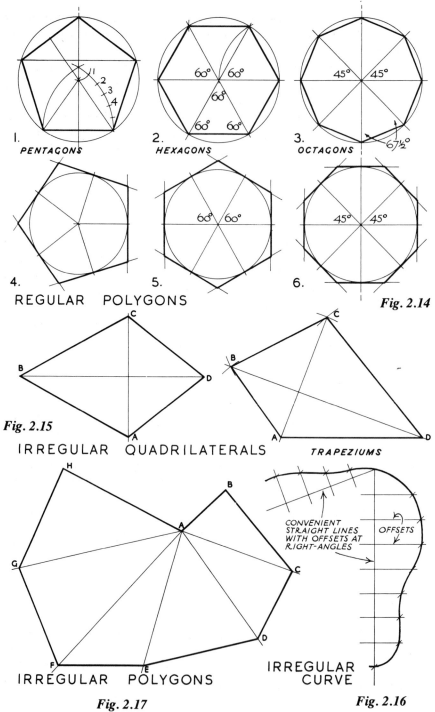

1. PENTAGONS

2. HEXAGONS

3. OCTAGONS

60° 60°
60°
60° 60°

45° 45°

67½°

4.   5.   6.

45° 45°
60° 60°

REGULAR POLYGONS

Fig. 2.14

IRREGULAR QUADRILATERALS

Fig. 2.15

TRAPEZIUMS

IRREGULAR POLYGONS

Fig. 2.17

CONVENIENT STRAIGHT LINES WITH OFFSETS AT RIGHT-ANGLES

OFFSETS

IRREGULAR CURVE

Fig. 2.16

the setting up can be done with the aid of a protractor or adjustable set square, the lengths of the lines being measured or transferred from an original by dividers.

If the lengths of the diagonals are known, the setting out can be made on the basis of triangulation. In the example illustrated, Fig. 2.15, side AD is drawn first; then, with centre A and radius equal to the length of the diagonal, an arc is drawn to intersect an arc drawn with centre D and radius equal to the length of known side DC. This establishes the position of point C, and by a similar process, using AC as the baseline, the triangle ABC can be drawn.

Irregular polygons

The drawing of an irregular polygon such as illustrated in Fig. 2.16 can be made on similar lines to the methods described above for irregular quadrilaterals. If the lengths of the sides and the angles between them are known, as is the case in the plotting of certain types of survey, the setting up is made by systematically measuring off lines and angles. If the lengths of the sides and the distances from one corner, point A here, to all other corners are known, the method is to construct the triangles so formed.

Irregular curves

The drawing of irregular curves, when copied from other drawings, is best done by plotting offsets from convenient straight lines that follow the general direction of the curve. This is illustrated in Fig. 2.17. The offsets are taken at right angles to the straight lines. They need not necessarily be spaced at regular intervals, although it is sometimes more convenient to do so.

If the curve is part of a survey, the lines and offsets will have been determined in the measuring, and the drawing is therefore a straightforward matter of plotting the data to scale.

Copying _____

Modern photocopiers are very versatile and capable of sophisticated enlargements and reduction.

An electric photocopier is capable of making same-size copies as well as reducing and enlarging line drawings made with an ink or a strong pencil line.

One can make good copy reductions from A3 to A4 and enlargements from A4 to A3. Also, other reductions and enlargements can be made by the use of preset percentages These reduced or enlarged copies can be made by placing the documents to be copied either in the document feeder or document handler bypass, or directly on the document glass.

There is also a copy contrast option built into the photocopier so that the copies may be lightened or darkened as required. (See Chapter 8 on photocopiers).

Enlargement and reduction of drawings _____

There are various methods of enlarging or reducing a line drawing.

If, for example, the drawing consists of irregular or complex lines, draw over it a square grid of light lines (or, if the drawing is to be protected, draw the grid on a piece of tracing paper and place over the original), and then for the new drawing make a similar grid but proportionately larger or smaller as required (Fig. 2.18 (1)). With this grid as a guide it is comparatively easy to make the copy to the size wanted.

If a line and its divisions, e.g. a scale, is to be enlarged or reduced in other than a simple mathematical proportion the method shown in Fig. 2.18 (2) is a useful method to employ. Line AB with points C and D along it is to be reduced; with centres A and B and radius equal to AB two arcs are drawn to intersect at O, and lines are drawn from O to A, B. C and D. The new length of the line is now measured along OA from O, and a line A'B' is drawn parallel to AB, to which it corresponds. Where this line cuts CO and DO points C' and D' corresponding to C and D on the original are found.

The proportional enlargement or reduction of rectangles is made by drawing a diagonal so that the alteration of the length of one side automatically gives the required length of the adjacent one. For example, in Fig. 2.18 (3) ABCD is the rectangle; BD is a diagonal. EFGD is a proportionately reduced rectangle.

Tracings done with soft pencil may be transferred to another piece of paper by shading the reverse image with a soft pencil and redrawing over the original image once again with an H or 2H pencil. Another way is to use a light table or box. A simple light box can be made by placing a sheet of strong glass over a drawer that contains a small light source.

Slide projectors are useful for enlargement purposes. A slide, when projected onto a screen, will blow up an image to almost any size desired. The enlarged image may then be traced in the usual way with either pen or pencil.

1.

2.

3.

PROPORTIONAL
COMPASSES

PANTOGRAPH

ENLARGEMENT
AND
REDUCTION

Fig. 2.18

3
Projections

Types of projection

Orthographic projection

Orthographic projection is the method of showing solid objects, which are actually three-dimensional, in two-dimensional drawings by means of related views called *plans, elevations* and *sections*. Most drawings of buildings are of this nature.

- A plan is a horizontal slice through the object to give an aerial view of the arrangements. It also generates the vertical section, the elevation and the axonometric projection (see later in this chapter).
- A section is a cross-cut made vertically through the form, which shows the way the interior space is organized.
- Elevations show the vertical planes derived from the plan, and retain their true size shape and detail in the same scale as the plan.

The principle is difficult to explain in words, but is readily understood when a drawing in orthographic projection is seen. It is illustrated in Figs. 3.1 and 3.2. Fig. 3.1 shows a block or rectangle prism, ABCDEFGH. Adjacent to it and parallel to its sides are three coordinated planes: that is, planes at right-angles to one another. They are the horizontal plane, vertical plane 1, and vertical plane 2. If the face of the prism ABCD is projected onto vertical plane 1 it appears thereon as a rectangle; similarly, if face EACG is projected onto vertical plane 2 it also appears as a rectangle; and likewise with face EFBA onto the horizontal plane. Now, if it is imagined that the coordinate planes are 'hinged', then if the horizontal plane is swung downwards, as it were, through an angle of 90°, and if vertical plane 2 is swung round through an.angle of 90°, the three projections will lie in the same plane and the result is as shown in Fig. 3.2, which is an *orthographic projection* of the prism showing related plan and two elevations.

In practice, of course, such a projection is made by drawing first the plan, then the elevation of the front face immediately above and then the end elevation at the side.

ORTHOGRAPHIC PROJECTION

Fig. 3.1

DIAGRAM TO SHOW
RELATED VIEWS OF
OBJECT OR BUILDING

DEVELOPMENT TO
BRING VIEWS INTO
ONE PLANE

Fig. 3.2

Sections

In addition to plans (horizontal views) and elevations (vertical views), onto which details are added, sections are also used in orthographic presentation in order to show further details of the interiors of buildings and the construction of walls, floors, etc. A section can be described as a view of a building or object seen when it has been cut straight through, usually in a horizontal or vertical direction.

Fig. 3.3 illustrates various sectional views. Assuming the rectangular prism, referred to above, to be hollow, if cut horizontally the view would be as in Fig. 3.3 (1). This view, properly termed a horizontal section, is usually called a *plan*. If cut longitudinally and vertically, (Fig. 3.3 (2)), the view is termed a *longitudinal* or *long section*. If cut across and vertically, (Fig. 3.3 (3)), diagram 3, it is called a *cross section*.

Of course there may be more than one of each type of section necessary and, according to the design of the building or object, several plans, elevations and sections may be required to show it fully. In drawing a building there is usually a plan (sectional plan) through each floor as well as of the roof and the foundations, elevations of all sides, and a number of sections taken at important positions.

Geometric solids

Fig. 3.4 shows various geometric solids represented by orthographic projection in plan, elevation and side elevation. Pictorial views are also shown so that the form in each case will be understood. It is important that the appearance of these solids in two-dimensional views should be fully appreciated as they are the basis of nearly all building forms. Exercises including these and other solids should be practised. Fig. 3.5 is such an example; the combination of geometric forms are those of the dome, drum and pendentives in building design. It will be seen that the sections are taken diagonally. Projection lines are shown so that the plotting of the curves can be followed.

Inclined cuts and true sections

Without going into detailed explanations of the plotting of them, Fig. 3.6 shows examples of six geometric solids drawn in orthographic projection cut by inclined planes at 45°. The true section or the new surface made by the cut is shown with a strong outline and is hatched in the pictorial view in each example.

SECTIONS

I.

HORIZONTAL SECTION
USUALLY CALLED 'PLAN'

2.

VERTICAL SECTION
LONGITUDINAL SECTION

3.

VERTICAL SECTION
CROSS SECTION

Fig. 3.3

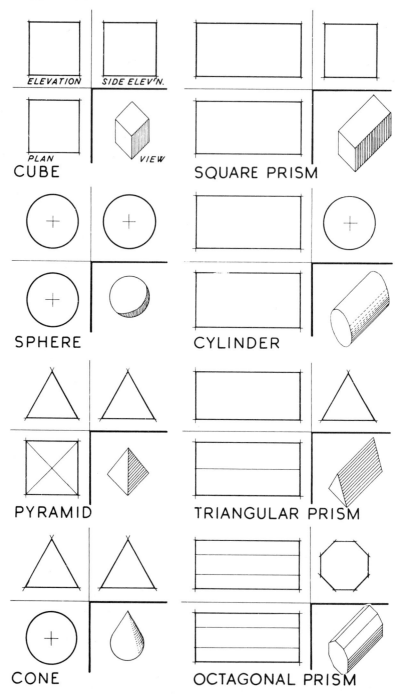

ELEVATION   SIDE ELEV'N.

PLAN   VIEW

CUBE

SQUARE PRISM

SPHERE

CYLINDER

PYRAMID

TRIANGULAR PRISM

CONE

OCTAGONAL PRISM

Fig. 3.4

Surface developments ─────────────────

It is sometimes necessary to show graphically the total surface area of a solid opened out as it were into one plane, e.g. shapes to cut in sheet metal or to be covered in some material.

Fig. 3.7 shows a number of simple geometric solids developed in this way The method is obvious in most cases. The surface of the cone is found by dividing the base on plan into a convenient number of parts and setting these off on an arc struck with its centre at the apex and radius equal to the inclined length in elevation. A similar method can be used for the cylinder, or the extent of the 'unrolled' area can be calculated by multiplying the diameter of the ends by p or 3.141.

Fig. 3.8 shows the method of finding the surface developments of the 'cloister' and 'cross' vault forms, pictorial views of which are given. The projection lines show how the diagonal sections are set up as well as how the developments are plotted.

Roof developments

Fig. 3.9 shows two examples of the graphical development of pitched roof surfaces, which are not represented in true proportion in ordinary orthographic projection, i.e. in plan and elevation. By following carefully the projection lines and noting the indexing, the way in which the developed, i.e. the actual, shapes of the surfaces are obtained will be understood. Pictorial views of the roofs are given to show their general appearance.

Similar exercises for various kinds of pitched roofs should be carried out as part of the study of geometrical drawing.

Spiral curves

Fig. 3.10 shows examples of the drawing of spiral curves.

1. A spiral about a cylinder or helix. This is the basis of the setting out of a spiral staircase. The cylinder is shown in plan and elevation. The circumference on plan is divided into a number of equal parts, indexed 0–12 in the example, and the height on elevation is marked with a number of equal divisions. By projecting up from the plan, points of intersection are found through which the spiral seen in elevation passes.
2. A spiral curve about a cone: this is a true spiral. The procedure to find the curve in elevation is similar to that for the cylinder. To find the curve on plan, draw concentric circles about the centre corresponding to the horizontal divisions on elevation. Join the points on the outer circumfer-

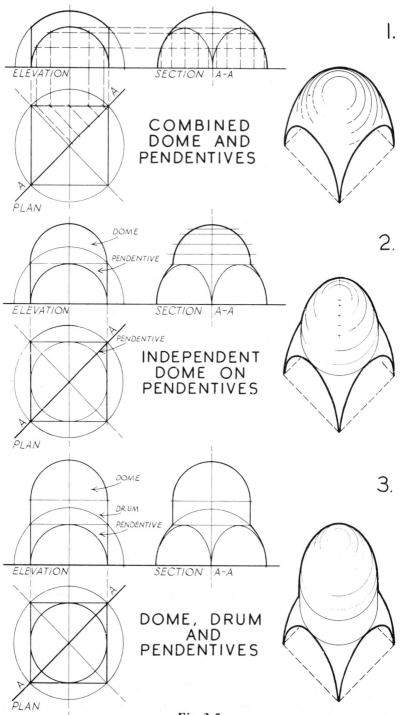

1.

ELEVATION   SECTION A-A

COMBINED
DOME AND
PENDENTIVES

PLAN

2.

DOME

PENDENTIVE

ELEVATION   SECTION A-A

PENDENTIVE

INDEPENDENT
DOME ON
PENDENTIVES

PLAN

3.

DOME

DRUM

PENDENTIVE

ELEVATION   SECTION A-A

DOME, DRUM
AND
PENDENTIVES

PLAN

Fig. 3.5

INCLINED CUT (45°)

TRUE SECTION

ELEVATIONS

PLAN

CIRCLE

ELLIPSE

ELLIPSE

CUBE OR SQUARE PRISM · SPHERE

ELLIPSE

PYRAMID · CONE

ELLIPSE

CYLINDER · OCTAGONAL PRISM

INCLINED CUTS AND TRUE SECTIONS

Fig. 3.6

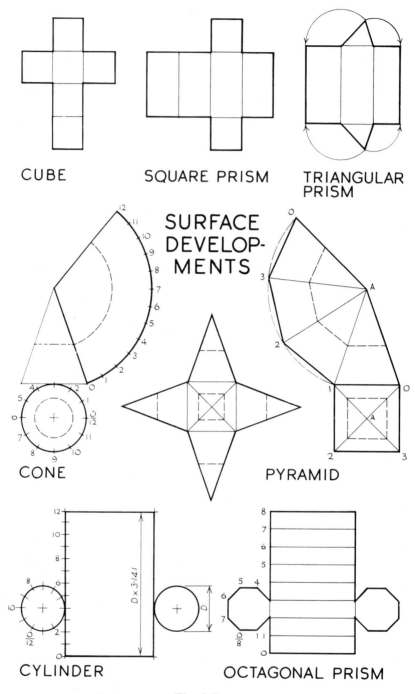

CUBE SQUARE PRISM TRIANGULAR PRISM

SURFACE DEVELOP-MENTS

CONE PYRAMID

CYLINDER OCTAGONAL PRISM

Fig. 3.7

ELEVATION   SECTION A-A

DEVELOPMENT
OF SURFACE

PLAN

'CLOISTER' VAULT FORM

ELEVATION   SECTION A-A

DEVELOPMENT
OF SURFACE

PLAN

CROSS VAULT FORM

Fig. 3.8

ROOF DEVELOPMENTS

Fig. 3.9

Fig. 3.10

ence on plan to the centre, and the curve can then be drawn through the appropriate intersections.

In addition to the various scrolls based on quadrants and the classical Ionic volute two other examples are:

3. The method is: Assume AB to be the greatest radii required or given; this is indexed 1. At right angles draw BC of convenient length and join A to C. Next, decide the number of radii to be used. This is a matter of judgment depending on the size of the scroll; 10 are taken here. Divide AB into ten equal parts. At the eighth part draw a line parallel to BC intersecting AC. From the intersection draw a perpendicular to BC: this gives radius 2. Join point 8 to C; where this line intersects radius 2 draw a line parallel to BC to intersect AC and so obtain radius 3. By continuing in this manner the series of radii can be obtained reduced in geometrical progression.

To draw the scroll with these radii, each one is used to describe a quadrant, as shown in Fig. 3.10 as far as radius 8.

4. A scroll drawn from four centres at the corner of a square by describing successive quadrants.

Axonometric projection

This contains the true plan. See Figs. 3.11 and 3.12. It can be set up by rotating the plan through 45°. The drawings can be made by a T-square and 45° set square, and so long as the 'plan' view remains a true plan, the angle of tilt can be varied to secure a good impression. Vertical lines are true in this projection. This projection is very useful for creating a 'birds-eye view' of a housing layout, particularly if the roads and landscaping are shown as well as the houses. Note that circles on plan are true circles but circles on elevation are shown as ellipses.

Isometric projection

This is similar to axonometric projection: the plan is a true plan, but this view is rather distorted if used as a 'birds-eye view'. Vertical lines are true in this projection. For some small construction details, isometric projection gives a realistic effect. The drawing is made with a T-square and a 30° set square. Circles appear as ellipses in plan and elevation. See Figs. 3.13 and 3.14.

AXONOMETRIC PROJECTION

Fig. 3.11

SET-SQUARE

AXONOMETRIC OF BRICK

QUARTER FULL SIZE

SET-SQUARE

90°   45°   45°   45°

ELEVATION

PLAN

AXONOMETRIC

HALF SCALE OF AXONOMETRICS

AXONOMETRIC

ELEVATION

PLAN

HALF SCALE OF AXONOMETRICS

AXONOMETRIC

AXONOMETRIC

VIEW LOOKING DOWN

VIEW LOOKING UP

AXONOMETRIC PROJECTIONS OF A STOOL

Fig. 3.12

Oblique projection

There are two variations of the method. In the first method, the oblique lines are drawn at 45° to the horizontal and vertical lines. In the second method, the oblique lines are drawn at 30° to the horizontal, and the same scale is used for oblique, horizontal and vertical lines. See Fig. 3.15.

Perspective projection

Perspective projection conveys an actual appearance of a building or object as a 3D image. Also, this projection recognizes the diminishing size of objects as they recede from the viewer. Setting up a perspective projection is somewhat complicated, but the important principle is to remember that the vanishing points are situated on the horizon (eye level) and all the horizontal lines of the projection are drawn back to the VP's. In a formal perspective projection the plan and elevation are the generators of the height and position of the 3D image. For further information on Perspective projection see Chapter 9.

ISOMETRIC PROJECTION

Fig. 3.13

SET-SQUARE

90°   30°   30°

ISOMETRIC OF BRICK

ISOMETRIC

ELEVATIONS

ORTHOGRAPHIC
PROJECTION -
HALF SCALE OF
ISOMETRICS

PLAN

ISOMETRIC

Fig. 3.14

ISOMETRIC

ELEVATION

PLAN

ORTHOGRAPHIC
PROJECTION -
HALF SCALE OF
ISOMETRICS.

ISOMETRIC

SET-SQUARE

HALF SCALE
FOR OBLIQUE — 4"
LINES — 3"
— 2"
— 1"

2" 1" 1"

FULL SCALE =
FOR
HORIZONTAL
& VERTICAL
LINES

90°   45°

2"

3"

T-SQUARE FOR
HORIZONTAL LINES

OBLIQUE PROJECTION OF BRICK
QUARTER FULL·SIZE

OBLIQUE PROJECTION

Fig. 3.15

ORTHOGRAPHIC
PROJECTIONS
(QUARTER SCALE
OF OBLIQUE
PROJECTIONS)

ELEVATIONS

PLAN

THREE DIFFERENT OBLIQUE VIEWS OF SAME OBJECT.

HALVED
JOINT

HALF LAP
JOINT

30°

COMMON JOINTS
IN CARPENTARY

OBLIQUE PROJECTIONS
30° ANGLE - FULL SCALE
FOR HORIZONTAL & VERTICAL
& OBLIQUE LINES.

MORTICE &
TENON

TENON

4
Lettering

Little progress can be made in architectural drawing without attention being paid to lettering.

Almost every drawing has to be titled, and many of them, particularly production drawings, require descriptive words and notes in order that they can be clearly understood. It is important, therefore, for the draughter of whatever category to acquire as quickly as possible the habit of using good lettering on all work. And as the study of lettering also, affords excellent practice in drawing it is particularly suitable that it should be dealt with at an early stage in the training.

With all lettering, the first principle is that of *legibility*. Legibility depends on (1) shape or form of each individual letter, (2) spacing of letters and arrangement of words, and (3) the sizes and positions of the lettering according to relative importance. The second principle is that of suitability of shape to materials and method of execution; thus lettering drawn in pencil on paper will differ in form to some extent from lettering incised in stone. Thirdly, the character of the lettering must be appropriate to its purpose. The type of letters and general composition of the wording should be expressive of the quality or use of the drawing: for example, decorative lettering is completely out of place on a working drawing, just as crude stencil lettering would be on a highly finished perspective drawing.

English lettering is derived from that of the Romans, and the generally accepted standard is the lettering that was carved on Trajan's Column, Rome, in the second century A.D. This lettering was probably first 'painted' on the stone with a brush and then incised with a chisel, which procedure accounts to some extent for the forms and details, such as the thick and thin strokes from the brush-work. and the 'serifs', originally the chiselled terminations of parts of the letters. Nevertheless, the forms have now become familiar in printing types, and flat letters and the Roman alphabet will always be the basis of good lettering.

The Roman alphabet

There is, however, no absolute standard for roman lettering, and many of the variations are not suitable for ordinary draughting purposes. The one shown in Fig. 4.1 has been specially prepared for drawings, bearing in mind the need for preserving the essential shapes and for a simple setting-out. It is an alphabet that should be carefully studied, and the best way to study it is to draw it out, for the basic proportions. It can be used for the titling of important drawings.

The construction of each letter is shown and should be understood on examination. These are some general points to note. First, all thin strokes are the same width, and all thick strokes – except the I and the J. which can be a little wider – are the same width. The thick strokes are about one-tenth the height of the letters; the thin strokes are rather more than half the thick strokes. Second, the letters are all one height except the 'points' of A, M, N. V and W. which extend, as do C, G, O and Q, a little beyond the limits in order to make them appear the right size (do not exaggerate this subtlety). Third, the middle line between the top and bottom guidelines determines the position of parts of several of the letters, as well as centres for C, G, O and Q.

Individual points are:

A Both sides inclined at 70°; the bottom of the crossbar is midway between the middle and bottom guidelines.

B Explained by drawing; construction lines are at 45°; centres of arcs are indicated by dots; arrows indicate radii.

C Outside curve is part of circle. inside curve is struck from centres indicated; axes at $22\frac{1}{2}°$ and $67\frac{1}{2}°$ to horizontal; widest parts rather wider than wide parts of thick strokes, same with G, O, and Q.

D Explained by drawing; note width of letter, about $\frac{3}{4}$ of height.

E Based on double square; note slight curve and slope of serif to top of lowest arm – same with L.

F Similar to upper part of E.

G Similar basis to C; note position of vertical stroke, determined by intersection of 45° line from centre with outside curve – compare with C.

H Explained by drawing.

I Explained by drawing.

J Centres for arcs can be judged by eye; curve must be smooth and regular.

K Curve to lower leg is drawn freehand, points must not become 'hook' – same with R.

L Similar to lower part of E.

M Explained by drawing.

N Explained by drawing.
O Similar construction to C
P Explained by drawing.
Q Similar construction to O, note positions along axis for centres of arcs for tail.
R Similar construction to P, but note junction of inner curve at top and junction between vertical stroke and leg; the leg should not be 'curly'.
S Explained by drawing; careful drawing necessary.
T Explained by drawing.
U Explained by drawing; foot can be omitted.
V, W. X, Y, Z explained by drawing.

It is only possible to use the setting-out fully if the letters are drawn to a reasonably large size. For small letters, while the angles can be followed, some parts have to be drawn freehand by eye instead of with compasses.

'Serifs' must be neatly formed and smoothly joined up with the rest of the letter, and should be put in before the final lines are completed.

Fig. 4.2 shows the stages in setting up three letters: (1) the guidelines and principal construction lines are drawn lightly; (2) the letters are lightly completed and the serifs drawn in freehand in the final line; (3) the letters are completed in the final line, curved lines being put in before straight lines in the case of B. *This procedure should be followed in general in making any drawing.*

The spacing of letters to form words can vary considerably within limits, depending upon space available, purpose, and so on. Because the individual letters differ in shape the spacing has to be arranged to avoid crowding in some parts of words and too wide spacing in others. Until the eye becomes trained a useful guide to spacing is given by the thick black lines shown under each letter in Fig. 4.1. The line in each case can be taken as representing the 'value' of the letter according to its shape and size; the letters are then spaced so that the distances between these value lines are equal, as illustrated by the word ROMAN. This method need not be rigidly adhered to; some variations may have to be made at times to suit circumstances.

Titles of important drawings should always be set out on tracing paper to get the size and spacing right before being drawn on the final sheets.

Sans-serif letters

In more recent times, letters without serifs, known as 'sans serif' alphabets, have been designed and are much used because of their simplicity, clarity and ease of execution. Fig. 4.3 shows the setting-out of such an alphabet[1]

[1]Based on Gill Sans, a printing type designed by Eric Gill for the Monotype Corporation

Fig. 4.1

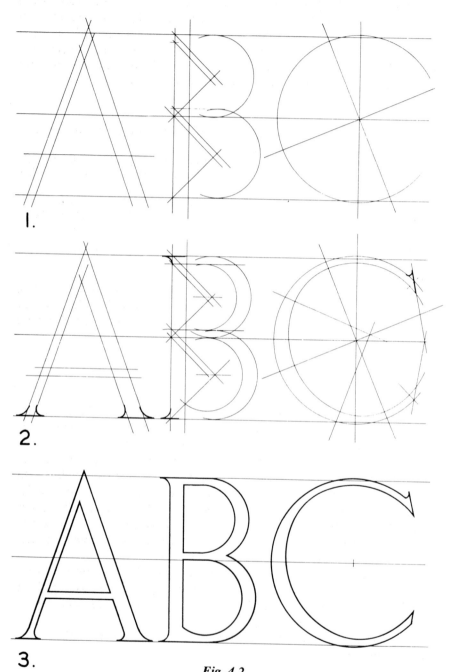

1.

2.

3.

Fig. 4.2

suitable for the titling of drawings, etc. The letters are formed of strokes all equal in thickness. Examples of these are shown in Fig 4.3 and below. One-tenth the height is an average thickness of the strokes, but it can be more or less according to the effect required. The thicker the stroke, the heavier or bolder the letter. The letters are all the same height. Suggested value lines for spacing are shown as in the case of the roman alphabet.

Dolmen, upper and lowercase, 20pt

Rundfunk, upper and lowercase, 20pt

Numerals

Fig. 4.4 shows the setting out of roman and sans serif numerals. Regarding the former, the Roman did not, of course, use numerals of this kind, which are Arabic in origin, but the character of roman lettering is followed and the shapes are based on those in common use for many years.

Single-line lettering

For habitual rapid use in labelling and putting notes on drawings, a single-line alphabet is required. This should be based on the shapes and proportions of the 'Roman' letters, but without the use of serifs.

Fig. 4.5 shows such an alphabet and corresponding numerals. In order to illustrate the shapes and proportions, guidelines dividing the height into eight equal parts and the centres of arcs are indicated. The lettering should, however, be drawn freehand at various sizes. It will be found, at first, that each letter has to be formed carefully and comparatively slowly to avoid distortion and wrong shapes. With practice, however, it is soon possible to letter quickly and accurately without conscious effort.

After a time certain individual characteristics will be acquired, but avoid the deliberate introduction of novel or fancy shapes in the mistaken idea that doing so imparts 'style'. Legibility and seemliness are far more important than individual idiosyncrasy.

Always rule faint guidelines for freehand lettering and keep to them. Use a reasonably soft pencil.

Fig. 4.3

ROMAN NUMERALS

'SANS' NUMERALS

Fig. 4.4

Inclined lettering

Sometimes it is necessary to distinguish between two types of lettering: for example, names of rooms on plan and notes regarding construction. While this might be effected by variations in size, it may be more convenient to use upright lettering for the one and inclined lettering for the other.

Fig. 4.6 shows inclined lettering similar in all respects otherwise to the single-line lettering above, but sloping uniformly at an angle of about 75°. The slope should not be exaggerated. Many draughters use inclined lettering for general use in preference to upright. It is a matter of personal choice.

Script lettering

Fig. 4.7 shows individually formed capitals, numerals and lower case letters, which can be written in pencil or pen. If well executed, script is an attractive way of labelling certain types of project presentation drawings.

A popular cursive pen lettering is italic script, which to the practised hand is a quick and neat style, particularly for groups of notes. There are a number of books that describe this writing, and it must be emphasized that legibility depends on careful forming of the letters in the accepted manner. Badly executed (often the result of excessive haste) or attempted at too small a size, this script degenerates into mere scribble, which is difficult to read and becomes a possible source of error, or at least a cause or irritation, to those who have to refer to the drawings concerned.

Broad pen lettering

This lettering (Fig. 4.8) is suitable for labelling drawings and for the more important general notes. It can only be done in ink, and special broad nibs of various sizes have to be used. Many kinds are available.

Lettering techniques _____

Stencil lettering

Stencilled letters can be used for titling drawings and are a means of achieving uniformity at negligible cost when a number of drawings are similarly titled. Fig. 4.9 shows an example and how the stencil is used. Stencils can be cut in thin metal but more often in clear plastic with either 'Roman' or block alphabets in a number of different sizes. The advantage of the clear

Fig. 4.5

ABCDEFGHIJKLMNOPQ
RSTUVWXYZ 1234567890

Fig. 4.6

ABCDEFGHIJKLMNOPQ
RSTUVWXYZ 1234567890
abcdefghijklmnopqrstuvwxyz

Fig. 4.7

ABCDEFGHIJKLMNOPQ
RSTUVWXYZ 1234567890
abcdefghijklmnopqrstuvwxyz

Fig. 4.8

plastic is that a guideline drawn on the paper can be seen through it. It is usually better to space out the letters fairly widely and regularly. Special stencil ink can be used or indian ink or opaque colour, etc. The brush must be almost dry, and the plate must be held down perfectly flat and firmly for good results.

The description 'stencil lettering' is also commonly applied – somewhat inaccurately in the author's opinion – to guided pen lettering.

Guided pen lettering

Fig. 4.10 shows examples of the letters produced by means of special pens and guides. Such lettering is used extensively for drawings of all kinds, particularly working drawings and details. Its popularity is due to its legibility, speed of execution, and the uniformity that it gives, especially when different draughters are working on the same set of drawings. Examples are also to be found in the illustrations used throughout this book.

Both upright and sloping guides are obtainable for capital, lower-case letters and numerals in a variety of sizes with corresponding pens. Drawing pens of the Rotring Isograph type can also be used.

Used carelessly, this lettering is as bad as the worst freehand, and a certain amount of practice is necessary to obtain lettering that is pleasing in appearance as well as very legible.
A few hints are:

- Only a small quantity of ink should be put in the pen. Keep the pen perfectly upright in use.
- Wash the pen out immediately after use and see that the wire is pushed well home.
- Keep the guides clean; do not let the ink clog the letters. A special cleaning liquid can be obtained for pens and guides.
- Always rule faint guidelines for letters, and consider the spacing before starting. Sometimes it may be advisable to make a trial setting-out.

Pressure-transfer lettering

This kind of lettering, also known as pressure sensitive, is extensively used on all kinds of architectural and planning drawings, particularly for titling and labelling. It is reasonably quick and most effective. Its only serious disadvantage is that it is rather expensive, especially as many letters of each sheet are never used.

The letters are printed on thin plastic sheets, usually 254 mm × 381 mm, although smaller sheets are available, in a variety of types of alphabets, numerals, punctuations, etc., and are protected by silicone-treated backing

ABCDEFGHIJKLM NOPQRSTUVWXYZ
1234567890 Nº &

ABCDEFGHIJKLM
NOPQRSTUVWXYZ

1234567890 Nº &

Fig. 4.9

ABCDEFGHIJKLMN
OPQRSTUVWXYZ
1234567890No/&

abcdefqhijklm
nopqrstuvwxyz
1234567890No

Fig. 4.10

sheets. A typical example is illustrated in Fig. 4.11. The characters can be applied to any smooth dry surface in any desired arrangement. Having decided on the type and size of letters to be used and estimated the placing on the drawing – this requires some experience – the technique of application is to remove the backing sheet and to position the first letter, on a previously ruled guideline if there are to be a series of letters, and then to 'shade' across the letter from top to bottom using a ball-point pen with moderate pressure. This action is continued until the letter appears lighter, which shows that it has been transferred to the surface of the paper. The lettering film is carefully peeled back until the letter is exposed; it is then moved to position the next letter and the transfer procedure is repeated. On completion of a word, or every few letters, even after each letter of the larger sizes, the backing sheet should be laid over and additional firm pressure applied by the finger, the edge of a scale, or a burnisher in order to obtain maximum adhesion. When application is made to tracing paper or film from which dyeline prints are to be obtained it may be necessary to spray the letters with a matt fixative or they will be damaged in the printing process. As the spray will also 'fix' any parts of the drawing on which it may fall, it is advisable to confine the area by masking.

Points continually to be kept in mind are: avoid accidentally pressing any other letter when making a transfer; keep sheets flat and unfolded and uncreased in a box, wallet or stout envelope away from excessive heat or humidity when not in use. However, the accidental transfer of a letter to drawing or tracing materials is not usually a serious matter as it can be removed by scraping gently with a razor blade. Incomplete letters can be patched by applying part of another letter or can be made good in indian ink.

Complete words such as PLAN, ELEVATION, EAST, WEST, etc., at a size suitable for the majority of production drawings, are available, as are N points, direction arrows, section lines, electrical symbols and other useful architectural characters. Special wording for repetitive use, title blocks, crests and indications of all kinds can be supplied to order where quantities warrant and the expense is justified. Every draughter should have a copy of a comprehensive catalogue or display sheet of the various standard pressure transfer alphabets for reference. The following types are suitable for general use:

Compacta or Helvetica
Labels – to agree with standard word sheets   – Grotesque 7 (36 pt)
Names of rooms and grouped notes   – Grotesque 209 (10 pt).

Examples are shown in Fig. 4.12 and elsewhere throughout this book.

Fig. 4.11   Transfer lettering: alphabets, numerals, words and symbols. (Reproduced by permission of Letraset Ltd; arrangement by author)

Optima ● ○

abcdefghijklmnopqrstuvw
ABCDEFGHIJKLMNOPQRS

Modern No. 20 ●

abcdefghijklmnopqrst
ABCDEFGHIJKLM
1234567890 &?!£$ (.,;:) »˝˜

Fig. 4.12

Miscellaneous

So far, we have dealt with lettering and techniques for more or less formal or finished drawings. For informal drawings and preliminary studies and sketches, effective use can often be made of felt- or fibre-tipped pens and markers in black or colours, or indeed in any medium that lends itself to a freer form of lettering. Legibility must never be sacrificed, but a flowing line with possibly some variations in thickness can impart interest and liveliness.

Notes on drawings

Notes on drawings are of two kinds: (1) those of a general nature, and (2) those that refer to some detail in particular. The former should be grouped, together in a suitable position and neatly arranged in panels of regular shape (Fig. 4.13).

They should be broken into paragraphs corresponding to the matters dealt with, for ease in reading. They should be as brief as possible consistent with clarity. Spacing should be considered in relation to balance and the scale of the drawing, but avoid cramping the letters and words or spreading them out so much as to make them illegible. The spaces between the letters should generally be less than the spaces between one line of notes and the next, otherwise the eye tends to read vertically, 'Chinese' fashion.

Detail notes should be reasonably small, 2–4 mm high, and neatly arranged close to the part of the drawing to which they refer. A short arrow as pointer should be all that is necessary to connect the note to the detail. Do not group detail notes if to do so means long 'snaky' arrows or lines to relate them to the drawing. Do not use 'keys' – that is, for example, numbering the rooms on a plan and then putting a list explaining what the numbers mean at the side of the drawing – unless lack of space or other reason makes such a course imperative, e.g. for certain kinds of coded drawings.

Words should only be underlined where special emphasis is required. Full-stops should not be used unless essential to the sense of the note.

Northpoints

The purpose of a northpoint on a drawing is to show the position of north in relation to the plan of a site or a building. It should therefore be on or near to the plan and should be clearly read: that is, be simple as well as accurate. Fig. 4.13 shows five typical examples, which are suitable for general requirements: the simple cross for sketches and production drawings and the V or arrow for design sheets. The letter 'N' should be shown in all cases.

NOTES

GENERAL NOTES SHOULD NOT BE SCATTERED OVER THE DRAWING BUT SHOULD BE NEATLY ARRANGED IN PANELS OF REGULAR SHAPE

THEY SHOULD BE BROKEN INTO PARAGRAPHS FOR EASE IN READING.

THE LETTERS AND WORDS SHOULD NOT BE CRAMPED NOR SO W I D E L Y SPACED AS TO BECOME ILLEGIBLE

TYPICAL NORTH POINTS

CONSTRUCTION LINES

FINISHED LINES

HIDDEN AND OVERHEAD DETAILS, ETC.

PROJECTION LINES

CENTRE LINES, AXES

BREAK LINES

R.S.Js., PIPE RUNS, ETC.

SECTION LINES

DIMENSION LINES

NCORRECT "

Fig. 4.13

Types of line

Fig. 4.13 also shows various lines used on drawings. Construction or setting-out lines are made as light as possible, and finished lines are strong and of even quality, as described previously.

Where it is required to show the lines of some object that is under or behind some other part or, in the case of plans, is above the level at which the plan is taken, broken lines consisting of regular short dashes separated by regular gaps are used, the lines being appreciably longer than the gaps. 'Dotted' lines should not be used.

Projection lines should be light like construction lines, but broken by regular gaps.

Centre lines or axes (axial lines) are usually shown by comparatively light continuous lines with a short gap and short line at each end. An alternative line for this purpose, recommended by the British Standards Institution, is one consisting of alternate long and short lines separated by regular gaps, as shown in the figure for overhead RSJs, etc. Centre lines should project a short distance beyond the outlines of the part to which they refer.

Where it is intended to show that a drawing is incomplete, break lines consisting of ruled lines with short zig-zags at intervals are used.

Section lines, which indicate where a plan has been 'cut' (see Chapter 2) are commonly shown by either of the ways illustrated. The black triangles or the placing of the letters show the way the sectional view is taken.

Dimension lines (see also page 120) should be lighter or thinner than outlines and should be continuous, not broken for the insertion of dimension figures. They should be terminated by arrowheads exactly touching the outlines or projection lines to which they relate, alternatively the dimension lines can be continued past the outlines and projection lines and the points of intersection emphasized by a small stroke or dot. Dimension figures should be placed immediately above the corresponding dimension line, either near the centre or at the extreme left. The figures should always be disposed along the line and not at right angles to it. Vertical dimension lines should have the figures on the left-hand side reading upwards.

Scales

When drawn scales are used – and it is the usual practice now not to do so unless the drawing is to be reproduced to a different size – they should be simple and easy to read. Two horizontal lines with appropriate vertical subdivisions and the words 'metres' and/or 'millimetres' is a satisfactory arrangement for metric drawings.

5
Drawings

Scale drawings

Most technical drawings are *scale drawings*: that is, the land, buildings or objects shown on them are not represented at their true size, but are larger or, more often, smaller in some proportion.

Fig. 5.1 is a scale drawing of a stool in the proportion of 1:10: that is, one-tenth fullsize. Note that the plan drawing consists of (1) a half-true plan looking down, and (2) a half-horizontal section through the legs. This method enables more details to be illustrated without repeating unnecessarily similar parts of the drawing. The sectional parts of the wood are defined more clearly by hatching between the outlines: see Chapter 7.

Fig. 5.2 shows a scale drawing of a small garage in orthographic projection consisting of plan, two elevations and two sections. The scale is 1:100. A pictorial drawing, not to the same scale, is included to show the general appearance of the garage. Note the representation of the brick walls on elevation by the horizontal lines of the courses, and of the vertical boarding of the doors. The conventional representation of certain other features, some of which occur here, is explained in the next chapter. As the drawing is not intended as a working drawing, however, constructional details are omitted.

Normally, drawings such as those just discussed would be made using an appropriate boxwood or plastic scale for marking off the required distances. Only if it were necessary to work to some unusual proportion would a scale have to be drawn at the outset by dividing a line into whatever units and subdivisions were required.

Types of drawing

The following notes describe drawings for certain purposes in connection with building and land development. The techniques of architectural drawing are in many respects common to all, but defined practice, including

ELEVATION

CROSS SECT.^N

750

350

30

PLANS

SCALE
DRAWING
OF A
STOOL

Fig. 5.1

FRONT ELEVATION   SIDE ELEVATION

LONG SECTION

2.400

5.000

2.500

PLAN

· BRICK WALLS
· REINFORCED CONCRETE ROOF
· WOOD DOORS
· STEEL WINDOWS
· CONCRETE FLOOR AND FOUNDATIONS

CROSS SECTION

SCALE DRAWING OF A SMALL GARAGE

1:100

Fig. 5.2

Table 5.1   Recommended scales (for use with the mteric system)

Use	Scale	Ratio
Maps	1 : 10000 000	1 mm to 1000 m
	1 : 5000 000	1 mm to 500 m
	1 : 200 000	1 mm to 200 m
	1 : 1000 000	1 mm to 100 m
	1 : 50 000	1 mm to 5 m
Town surveys	1 : 50 000	1 mm to 50 m
	1 : 20 000	1 mm to 20 m
	1 : 10 000	1 mm to 10 m
	1 : 5000	1 mm to 5 m
	1 : 2500	1 mm to 2.5 m
Survey and layouts	1 : 2500	1 mm to 2.5 m
	1 : 2000	1 mm to 2 m
	1 : 1250	1 mm to 1.25 m
	1 : 1000	1 mm to 1 m
	1 : 500	1 mm to 0.5 m
Site and key plans	1 : 1250	1 mm to 1.25 m
	1 : 1000	1 mm to 1 m
	1 : 500	1 mm to 0.5 m
Sketch schemes, etc.	1 : 200	1 mm to 0.2 m
	1 : 100	1 mm to 0.1 m
Operational drawings	1 : 200	1 mm to 0.2 m
	1 : 100	1 mm to 0.1 m
	1 : 50	1 mm to 0.05 m

conventional representations and indications, vary for each profession, and reference should be made to current accepted standards and methods, and to specimens and examples of contemporary work.

Planning drawings

In this category are survey maps and diagrams made to show existing topography, buildings, communications, etc., preliminary designs on broad lines to show proposed new development, statutory scheme maps, detailed layouts and townscape studies (Fig. 5.3). Many planning drawings are prepared on or over Ordnance sheets, some of which may have to be brought up to date. As the scales are often small, minor slips can be serious and great care should be taken with such drawings. Draughtsmanship must be precise.

Particulars of standard notations and representations for official survey

Table 5.2 Comparison of metric and and imperial (foot/inch) scales

Scales for use with metric system	Scales for use with foot/inch system	
1:1 000 000	1:1000 000	$\frac{1}{16}$ in to 1 mile approx.
1:500000	1:625 000	$\frac{1}{10}$ in to 1 mile approx.
1:200000	1:250 000	$\frac{1}{4}$ in to 1 mile approx.
1:100000	1:126 720	$\frac{1}{2}$ in to 1 mile
1:50000	1:63 360	1 in to 1 mile
1:20000	1:25 000	$2\frac{1}{2}$ in to 1 mile approx.
1:10000	1:10 560	6 in to 1 mile
1:5000		
1:2000	1:2500	1 in to 208.33 ft
1:1000	1:1250	1 in to 104.17 ft
1:500	1:500	1 in to 41.6 ft
	1:384	$\frac{1}{32}$ in to 1 ft
1:200	1:192	$\frac{1}{16}$ in to1 ft
1:100	1:96	$\frac{1}{8}$ in to1 ft
1:50	1:48	$\frac{1}{4}$ in to 1 ft
1:20	1:24	$\frac{1}{2}$ in to 1 ft
1:10	1:12	1 in to1 ft
1:5	1:4	3 in to1 ft

and development plan maps in Britain are given in circulars and other publications of the Department of the Environment. These directives and guides[1] have been prepared not only to achieve uniformity and clarity but also with regard to ease and economy in the reproduction of plans, many copies of which are often required. Boundaries, communications, services, and other information covering planning concepts and proposals are expressed by means of various cross-hatching, edgings and by letters and combinations of letters related to an alphabetical index. Specimen maps are included to illustrate these representations and annotations to various scales with and without additional conventional colours, and to describe methods of preparing plans for printing in stages.

In the design process, preliminary planning studies are often made on tracing paper over maps in freehand, using soft pencils or felt pens. Strong black outlines and shadings are used, and distinctive colours employed for emphasis. Lettering is free and flowing whether in ink or pencil, and various 'shorthand' symbols project ideas and explore possible solutions and, if required, convey them to other members of the planning team Alternatively, similar but more diagrammatic sketches may be made on detail paper in coloured chalks.

Developed design drawings may be more carefully made over maps on tracing media in ink outlines, with rules, hatchings and transfer lettering for

[1]In particular *Development Plans: A Manual of Form and Content*, HMSO, 1970.

Fig. 5.3   Example of drawing of part of town plan showing proposed redevelopment indicated by various edgings, hatchings, letters etc. (Reproduced by permission of Hertfordshire County Planning Officer)

photoprint reproduction to which mechanical tones and conventional colours can be added. Such drawings will show, according to scale, appropriate detailed indication of buildings, roads, trees, planting, etc. Trees, incidentally, may be put on negatives or prints by standard transfer sheets as described in Chapter 4. Axonometric and isometric drawings of building masses may supplement plans and sections, as may perspectives individually prepared or derived from computer techniques.

Townscape drawings in further explanation of planning proposals or as part of environmental architectural presentation can be made in a variety of techniques according to the subject or scene to be depicted and the purpose of the illustration. A reasonable free style, using pencil or pen-and ink lines with monochrome or coloured washes may be appropriate, or a more formal drawing and rendering may be better suited to the subject. There is considerable scope for imaginative expression without loss of accuracy or realism.

Landscape drawings

Landscaping covers a wide range of work in connection with outdoor environment, from the conservation and management of regional areas to the laying out and planting of small spaces between buildings. Drawings of various kinds are employed. Broadly classified, they fall into three groups corresponding to general procedure: site analysis and preliminary, main report, and working drawings.

In the first category there are drawings made over existing maps, new survey drawings showing contours and topographical details, and sketches of the terrain and its surroundings, followed by drawings, freehand in the main, to illustrate preliminary outline proposals. Any appropriate technique may be used, and coloured pencils and felt-tipped pens with simple hatchings and basic indications can quickly produce concept drawings and help to develop ideas.

Drawings to accompany a main report, which are communications between designer and client, require to be of a more finished nature, using conventional and easily understood representations and techniques. The drawings should be fully annotated with cross-references as necessary. Plans should be to scale. There is an advantage in making them to the same scales as subsequent working drawings, but to do so may involve more draughting time and detail work than justified at this stage. Generally, drawings need be no bigger nor more in number than adequate to show the intended work. Elaborate drawings will not compensate for weak or undeveloped designs, although scruffy drawings may obscure good ideas. Sections may be required to show changes in ground levels, sight lines, etc., and perspective sketches will help in conveying the character of the completed design or the effect of various proposals. Use can be made of bold arrows, broken lines, lines of different thicknesses, shading and colour to clarify the design.

Working drawings may be less exact than building or planning drawings, but nevertheless they should be set out with reasonable accuracy from maps or surveys. For very large sites, drawing techniques may well follow civil engineering practice, for example in regard to major earthworks, or drainage schemes. For even more extensive areas, standard map notations may be adopted, perhaps with a key master plan related to detail drawings. For general construction purposes, drawings should be made in accordance with the current British Standard specification BSS 1192 Part 4(1984).

Trees are usually represented by plain or serrated circles, which may be drawn by compasses but more quickly through a template, unless of special significance, when a more literal representation may be used. Diameters should be approximately to scale and the trees accurately placed in their positions. Letters or numerals are commonly used to relate each tree to a legend giving the botanical name, which is usually too long to be repeated, and other particulars. On larger drawings the actual positions of tree trunks may be located by dimensions, although it is usual for the setting out of new planting to be made on site. Hedges and other planted areas can be similarly shown by a strong serrated outline, distinction being made between main and under plantings. Grassed areas can be indicated by dots or by an applied mechanical pressure transfer tint or colour. Roads, fencing, boundaries, car parking, bollards, water, etc. all have appropriate indications. Drawings can be made on white or coloured paper, or on tracing media for reproduction. Working drawings should be fully dimensioned and have north points and scales clearly marked. Titles and notes should be clear and unaffected.

Conveyance and lease plans

Drawings are used to assist in the identification of land or property in connection with sales and leases. The drawings are usually attached to and form part of the legal documents.

Boundaries should be clearly and accurately shown. In the case of building plots the frontages, depths and widths at the rear should be dimensioned in metres or millimetres. As individual plots are usually traced from a survey plan of the estate it is essential that the latter is correct in all respects and that the tracing is carefully made. Where natural boundaries do not exist, tie-measurements to the nearest road should be shown and dimensioned. Ownership of and responsibility for the maintenance of fences, etc., is indicated by 'T' marks (see Fig 5.4). Double 'Ts' indicate shared responsibility.

Colours are used to show the land conveyed, usually crimson lake or burnt sienna, and any part over which a right of way is granted, usually blue.

Descriptive lettering should be neat and legible. North points must always be shown, as reference to cardinal points is frequently made in the wording of the documents.

Measured drawings

These scale drawings are made from carefully taken measurements of existing buildings of historic interest and architectural merit as part of students' training in design and, to an increasing extent, for purposes of recording such works (especially in connection with preservation and conservation under Town Planning legislation and the requirement of English Heritage) and also any building to which alterations, additions or restorations are to be made (Fig. 5.5). The drawings may illustrate a whole building or part of a building and may range from small-scale plans and elevations to full-size details.

Space here does not allow a full description of the various types of subject and their presentation. Sometimes, form or decoration is the chief interest; in other cases constructional features are of most importance. Technique must vary accordingly, but elaborate rendering is generally unnecessary. The more direct the exposition the better, with special care being taken in regard to freehand detail, titles and lettering. Accuracy, of course, a first essential, should be of the highest. Drawings mainly in pencil with outlines of plans and sections in ink and perhaps with openings and conventional shadows in wash are usually satisfactory. Part plans and sections are often superimposed over corresponding details shown in elevation. The scale and north point should always be shown prominently and descriptive notes should be well arranged.

In making the survey of a building, the first step is to make a series of diagrammatic sketches (see Chapter 11) on which the necessary measurements can be marked. The importance of these sketches cannot be overemphasized. They should be made in suitable stiff-backed sketch-books or on clipboards on thin but tough plain paper, preferably not less than A3 size. Complicated work is best plotted to a small scale as the measuring proceeds.

Sketch measured drawings are carefully made sketches in pen or pencil, often in perspective and sometimes with approximate scale details added, on which overall main measurements are shown by lines and arrows.

CONVENTIONAL INDICATIONS
FOR SURVEY DRAWINGS

Fig. 5.4

MAIDS OF HONOUR ROW RICHMOND

Fig 5.5 Students measured drawing of building of historic interest. Pencil and water colour wash with conventional shadows.

Architectural drawings _____

The range of architectural drawings is considerable, and despite efforts at standardization there are widely differing techniques and styles used in their preparation. The following is a broad classification of the main types.

Preliminary

This includes graphic interpretation of sites and site conditions, feasibility studies, i.e. investigation and analysis of the building's requirements (brief), and the working out of main lines of possible design solutions. Such drawings are generally 'short life' drawings, sometimes little more than diagrams or rough sketches, and are usually made freehand, often on gridded paper or over gridded boards or backing sheets, although where appropriate they may be set up to small scales using T-square and set square. Simple perspectives may also be made at this stage, and for environmental studies or discussions with clients and others, surroundings and shadows can be indicated.

Sketch designs, which are part of architectural training, are somewhat similar to the above but, as well as planning exercises, they include a large proportion of design problems of a more imaginative kind, calling for the rapid and effective presentation of solutions usually in perspective. Usually not more than six hours are allowed for the preparation of such drawings and the presentation must therefore be on broad lines without overmuch attention to detail; the suggestion of the essential qualities of the design, construction and general character is all that is required. Freedom of technique is imperative, and the opportunities should be taken for experiments in appropriate media, such as soft pencil, crayon, charcoal, pastel and poster colour, and in the using of various papers, including coloured and textured papers.

Design

This includes drawings made for the development of designs, which in certain cases require the collaboration of consultants and specialists such as structural and mechanical engineers; draft constructional details; and complete design drawings which may be highly finished. Development drawings can vary greatly in techniques and scales according to the purposes for which they are prepared, e.g. for the putting down of the designers' thoughts ('ideograms' or concept drawings) and conversely for graphic representation to stimulate new ideas, to help forward stage by stage the logical process of designing and to provide a means of communication between members of the design team. Depending upon the size and

Fig. 5.6 Proposed shopping development in Weymouth (author Jim Mark MSA I).

type of a particular project, there may be many such drawings, most of which are made on tracing paper and have a relatively short life.

Finished design drawings show a minimum of constructional detail, although the construction must be fully worked out before they can be properly completed. In practice it often happens that after agreement has been reached on a preliminary sketch design, the next step is the preparation of production drawings with such modifications as may be necessary, and finished design drawings are not made until later, if at all. The designs of students, however, are usually required to be shown fully on well-finished presentation drawings.

In all cases the drawings may be orthographic projections, metric projections, or perspectives accurately drawn and effectively rendered. The layout of the sheets is important, and care must be taken to avoid crowded and unbalanced arrangements. Dimensions should not normally be shown, nor should notes of materials – except as footnotes – nor structural details on plan and section unless required for some special purpose.

Conventional shadows may be shown (see page 178) in order to explain the forms, etc., and appropriate surroundings can be included. The degree of formality or freedom of the presentation will depend upon the character of the subject and the use to which the drawing will be put. Lettering in particular must be carefully arranged and executed in a suitable alphabet. It will be confined in the main to the title, labelling of plans, elevations and sections, names of rooms, etc., and possibly some brief general notes.

Colour design drawings are usually orthographic or axonometric projections of the interiors of rooms, and serve both to show the design and to guide the execution of the actual work. Colours should therefore be as near as possible to those to be used. Flat opaque hues should be used for painted areas. Designers' colours, poster colours, ordinary water-colours or artists coloured pencils and crayons, and pastels can be used.

Production

Formerly described as 'working drawings', production drawings are made for the purpose of conveying precise constructional information, e.g. for the use of quantity surveyors; in combination with other documents, for obtaining planning and building regulations approvals, for obtaining tenders or negotiating contracts, and for instructing contractors and other members of the building team. They are invariably drawn in final form on good-quality tracing paper or film, usually in pencil with some ink work and applied lettering, but sometimes wholly in ink, for reproduction by photoprinting processes. The negatives are valuable documents to be handled and stored with care.

The drawings are generally orthographic projections to scale – an appropriate ratio being used according to size and purpose – although metric projections may also be included to explain detail construction. Arrangement of each sheet should be well organized, and for each job drawings should be standard in size, and uniform in technique, annotation, dimensioning, references, etc.

The typical set of traditional production drawings, which are still extensively used particularly for smaller buildings, comprises complete plans, elevations and sections drawn to a scale of 1:100 or 1:50 and details to larger scales ranging from 1:20 to fullsize, on which more or less total construction is shown. Negative prints are sometimes made of the basic plans and on these are added services such as electrical, sanitary, and heating and ventilating layouts. The drawings are supplemented by door and window schedules, etc. The method has the advantage of conveying information by comparatively few drawings of a kind better understood by the less sophisticated building firms: both in the drawing stage and on the site the relationships between adjoining and interconnecting elements can be more readily grasped. However, with the increasing complexity of construction, a multiplicity of lines and lettering can cause confusion and error, a situation worsened if changes are made during the progress of the works.

To overcome this problem, where larger projects are concerned, drawings can be made on an operational or elemental basis. Master layouts, e.g. structural grids, are prepared, and on negative prints thereof the work of one trade or one subcontractor only is shown on each drawing. This enables operational information to be quickly and clearly conveyed, and facilitates job information. Disadvantages are the greatly increased number of drawings required for each job, and the tendency for omissions and lack of coordination to occur unless particular care is exercised, as of course it should be, in making and checking the drawings.

No shadows or shading other than the indication of materials, and no extraneous details not relevant to the construction should be shown. A 'busy' working drawing in which every detail is drawn elaborately and repeated unnecessarily has no advantages and may be illegible. Lettering must be clear and tidily arranged, particularly as it may constitute half the drawing. Nevertheless, it must be kept as brief as possible, and any general notes should not be expanded to long clauses belonging properly to the specification.

General layout of drawings

These notes apply to all types of drawing, but are made with special reference to architectural drawings.

Sizes of working drawings and site plans should conform to the standard dimensions referred to previously, page 19, but architectural design drawings and students' exercise drawings need not necessarily be standardized. Fig. 5.7 shows a suitable layout for the last-named, providing spaces for title, student's name, and date, mark, etc. Some such layout is advisable for early geometry, construction and similar sheets.

Fig. 5.8 shows the layout of design drawings. Titles are usually best placed towards the bottom of the sheet and should be symmetrically disposed if the arrangement as a whole is otherwise symmetrical, but the title must always be included as part of the composition of the drawing, and it may therefore be advisable to place the title in some other position. The title must never be 'mean' or out of keeping with the character of the subject. The name of the designer(s) and draughters should appear in the bottom right-hand corner unless forming part of the title. Borders should be simple and neatly drawn, consisting of two or three ruled lines with perhaps a band of colour.

They are helpful in pulling together a loosely composed sheet, but are not essential.

Fig. 5.9 shows a type of layout for contract and production drawings, which is standard practice. Such a standard arrangement makes easier the reading of drawings, makes it possible for essential references to be located without trouble – an important point when drawings are prepared in several offices for one job – and reduces the likelihood of essential information being omitted. The placing of general and revision notes in a panel immediately above the name panel makes them readily seen if the drawings or prints are bound together or folded.

Fig. 5.10 shows a detail of a revision panel and name block, which may be drawn, stamped, preprinted or applied.

Titles of jobs and descriptions of drawings should be as brief as possible. The title should not be varied on different drawings relating to the same work, nor during the progress of the contract. If the drawings or prints are to be bound together, as shown in Fig. 5.11, it is probably better to have the title and sheet number in the top right-hand corner; if the sheets are to be kept loose in the drawers of a plan chest, the title, etc., is more readily seen if put along the bottom.

Fig. 5.12 shows the arrangement of a typical 1:100 scale working drawing of a small house on a standard sheet laid out as shown in Fig. 5.9. Further details of the plans, elevation, sections, etc., are given in Figs. 7.27–7.39 in Chapter 7.

GENERAL LAY-OUT OF STUDENT'S EXERCISE
DRAWING   NORMAL DRAWING PAPER SIZES.

Fig. 5.7

GENERAL LAY-OUT OF DESIGN DRAWINGS
NORMAL DRAWING PAPER SIZES

Fig. 5.8

GENERAL LAY-OUT OF WORKING DRAWINGS

Fig. 5.9

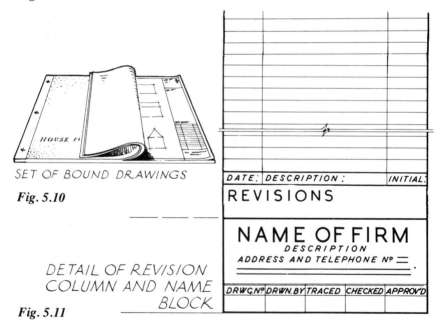

SET OF BOUND DRAWINGS

Fig. 5.10

DETAIL OF REVISION
COLUMN AND NAME
BLOCK

Fig. 5.11

View A

3 Deemed-to-satisfy examples

These examples show imaginary projects that conform to these standards. They do not show preferred solutions. Their purpose is to illustrate to developers the type of housing environment which they might create using these standards, and to show the potential within the constraints.

Diagram 3.1 is part of an estate with a collector road coming off the local distributor. Varying numbers of houses are grouped around access ways with a secondary footway system which would link play spaces, shops, bus stops, etc. These footways and back boundaries are suitable places for planting forest trees.

Fig. 5.13 Black and white drawings from design guide. Freehand drawing above with interesting tree delineation and texture tone for roadway. Plan to right uses transfer tone for minor access roads, transfer trees, and dots indicating footways. (Reproduced from Planning Department 1973, with permission of the Department)

LAY-OUT OF DRAWING   **Fig. 5.12**   DRAWING OF SMALL HOUSE

FLOOR PLAN

SCALE 1:50

Fig 5.14   A simple plan drawn by the computer using techniques similar to those described in Chapter 6.

Fig. 5.15 A carefully executed and accurate representation of orinignal elevational design set up from site measurements. Facade of Nos 56 and 58 Queens Gate Terrace, Kensington, London. Drawn in black ink and pencil on smooth white surfaced board by John Sambrook. (reproduced by permission of the Greater London Council from their Survey of London)

Fig. 5.16   One of the on-site plottings made during the measuring of Nos 56 and 58 Queens gate Terrace (see Fig. 5.15). Measured and drawn by John Sambrook.

6
Computer Graphics and Design

Considerable advances have been, and are being made, in the use of computers as aids in architecture and building. The architectural profession is acquiring and using these new tools. Apart from the rapid carrying out of complex calculations, computers are now being used to process information and are influencing the draughting of graphics. Computer graphics and computer-aided design (CAD) systems have been in existence since about 1970 and can now be used for drawing and modelling. Computer graphics and design systems are now available for draughters and designers.

From experience gained from measurements and performance standards of particular types of building, e.g. schools, hospitals, and airports, integrated suites of computer programs can be developed relevant to the outline proposal stage, comprising analyses of accommodation, generation of layouts, and appraisals in economic, functional and environmental terms. Much of this can be graphically expressed by diagrams and drawings produced on normal tracing detail paper, using conventional drawing pens and ink, and in most respects they are analogous to corresponding manually produced graphic representations.

At town planning level, appropriate programs have been devised for the purpose of aggregating population maps and optimally to locate such central facilities as schools and shops, as well as for the study of land use possibilities, e.g. the provision of residential, recreational and other major areas.

An understanding of computer graphics and CAD is becoming an essential requirement for some draughters. Drawing with a computer requires a different attitude as well as a different set of skills to the traditional approach to drawing. Drawing with a computer can save time and produce more drawings in a day than might be produced in a week by traditional methods. Apart from producing high-quality graphics, another use of CG and CAD is to link these graphics to constructional details, lists of materials, specifications, cost data etc.

The acquisition of computers (hardware) and the programes (software) is within the capabilities of most modern design offices today, and there is now a wide range of proprietary CG and CAD systems on offer, which have been developed independently using varying terminology as well as storing data in different ways.

In the 1980s computers became less complicated and less expensive than earlier models, and more recently there have been developments that have offered designers an exciting opportunity of draughting in a more realistic way. These programes are either: (1) derived from 2D CAD pro-grammes or (2) those that model directly in 3D. The first type is probably more useful to architects, being related to a system of dimensional units that is familiar to them. The second type offers great design possibilities in 3D for producing and testing ideas as well as having great value in bringing the reality of a design closer, before it is built. Again, simulated movement through a model is possible by simple animation, which enables designers to visualize the significance of their designs, as well as a means of communi-cating the 3D character of their design to others.

These factors have created a lot of interest and some concern among the users because of the choice, price, versatility and compatability of different systems available. The following is an attempt to explain and define the terminology used in computer graphics and design.

A definition of computer graphics _____

In computer language, a collection of organized information is called a database. A drawing is highly organized information which can be electronically stored as numbers representing points, lines, angles, etc in the computer memory.

It should be noted that there is a distinction between computer graphics and CAD. In the case of CAD, computer graphics has generated a design outcome, in the same way as drawings done by traditional methods often (although not necessarily) form the basis of an intended design outcome. Again, it must be stressed that computer graphics may be employed for the production of other illustrative material such as graphs, diagrams, and mis-cellaneous graphic material.

For a definition and explanation of computer graphics the following is recommended:

- *Creation of* relates to the scanning of images, the construction of objects and model building using data put into the computer.
- *Manipulation of* is the accessing, modifying and transforming of these objects.

- *Analysis of* is the processing that produces objects and their properties from mathematical, topological and geometric analysis.
- *Pictorial representations of objects* means not only pictures but also diagrams, maps, plans, etc.

The computer program

The computer program, also called the *software*, is a set of instructions written in computer language that tells a computer to perform certain tasks. Software is generally stored on disk and allows each piece of information to be recalled or modified to create a drawing electronically that can be printed on paper or reproduced on a printer or a plotter. For example, in order to produce a drawing or model of a building by computer, a two- or three-dimensional mathematical model of the building is created by the computer after data has been input.

Specific systems do this in a variety of ways, and most systems are variations on a similar data structure process. A data structure that has been derived from a number of proprietary computer graphics and CAD packages with a standard terminology can be related to many of the system-specific terms in use. Users should familiarize themselves with the characteristics of their own system and acknowledge the differences with others if exchange of data is envisaged.

The computer model

The computer model of a building, part of a building or a group of buildings comprises a set of entities that are called *primitives* or *instances*. These are the fundamental units of computer graphics, and there should be a wide range to allow for complicated forms and shapes to be drawn by the computer.

A typical range of primitives should include:

- arcs
- circles
- conics
- dimensioning
- grids
- hatching
- line styles
- lines
- planar shapes
- polygons
- polyhedra

- rectangles
- spheres
- splines
- strings
- text

Generally

System users should have a basic understanding of how their system structures and manipulates raw data. This may involve the use of some training.

Drawing and draughting in the traditional manner are based on skills that involve placing lines together to create finished drawings using techniques described in the other chapters of this book. With computer graphics and CAD the approach is more related to seeing graphic images in terms of patterns and assembling these standard patterns to form finished drawings. This enables patterns to be stored in the computer memory for future use. Simply put these standard patterns and objects can be recalled from the computer memory and reassembled and repeated to form further drawings, thus saving the draughter's time and enabling a certain amount of mass production.

Manual drawings are small-scale representations of large objects. Computers see drawings as full size and only after the plotting has taken place is the drawing stretched or reduced to any preferred scale.

Two-dimensional drawings produced by the computer are based on an x and y axis coordinate system. Three-dimensional drawings add a third z axis, which extends above and below the origin. The display screen of computer graphics and CAD is smaller than the size of typical drawing paper, and because draughters are working at full size this may create some difficulties at first as they adapt to the new system.

Two-dimensional drawings can be produced by the computer with the aid of appropriate software. Three-dimensional drawings can also be produced by projecting simple two-dimensional drawings into a third dimension. These perspective images are often displayed as 'wire frame' shapes and lines, and are used to delineate surface shape and form. Likewise, axonometric projections can be produced to give a 'bird's-eye view' of the drawing. These three-dimensional drawings can also be rotated and transformed as required.

Program compatibility and exchange

Before using CAD, it is necessary to use a 'foundation' program called an *operating system*. This informs the computer how to use its memory, data storage and peripheral equipment. Many computers use an operating system called MS-DOS or a more powerful system called Unix, which incorporates MS-DOS.

It is important to note that programs that are run on the same computer do not necessarily produce files that are mutually compatible. Some programs include additional facilities for translating drawings and data into intermediate formats that can be read by other programs. The most widely used format for this is IGES (initial graphics exchange specification). Another one is the AutoCAD DXF interchange file format, which may be read by many other programs. This latter format has become an accepted means of exchanging CAD data between different CAD programs. Again, an international standard known as STEP is already being used to control the format of data about products to allow easy interchange but this has yet to pass into the construction world.

Another useful feature is the way in which groupings of similar drawing elements may be manipulated together by the use of *layers*. This is analogous to the use of tracing paper overlays in manual drawing except that the groups of layers may be managed together, as if they could be combined into a single sheet, then separated. Layers in CAD are extremely useful in assisting the construction of a drawing or model.

CAD also has the ability to import (include) and to reference (display but not include) other drawings within an existing drawing.

Lastly, a graphics program informs the computer how to deal with drawing elements. The program then goes on to inform the computer how to produce images on a visual display, a printer or a plotter. Then the computer graphics or CAD program provide a series of commands to allow the user to manipulate the elements.

Hardware for computer graphics

It is important for the user to be familiar with different types of computer and the peripherals. The 'brain' of the computer is the *central processing unit* (CPU). In the 1970s, CPU's were housed in wafer-sized silicon chips, which could store and process information effectively, and these chips helped to develop microcomputers and personal computers

Storing and retrieving information

There are two ways of storing graphic information:

1. on silicon chips within the computer which is a working memory within the computer random access memory and which is lost when the machine is turned off.

2. removable floppy disks, which are used to store data for future use. A floppy disk can be used repeatedly, carried from one computer to another and is capable of storing a good deal of graphic information.

Hard disks are used for the storage of mass media and are necessary for computer graphics and CAD. Hard disks are not removable and are a fixture within the computer. Hard disks have a greater capacity and are faster than floppy disks. A hard disk will contain the programs and the drawings as well as additional information regarding estimating costs etc.

Display screen

The display screen is what the draughter will be watching most of the time so it should be easy to look at. This display comprises a box called a monitor, which has within it the cathode-ray tube. Also included is the graphic adapter housed within the computer and whose function is to use the electronic messages from the program, changing them into graphics and displaying them onto the monitor. Not all monitors, adapters and programs are necessarily compatible.

The monitor's size can vary from 13 in to up to 25 in depending on the resolution, i.e. the number of dots displayed horizontally and vertically on the screen. The range is from 640×350 (the minimum) to over 1280×1024.

Fig. 6.1   A typical workstation

The higher the resolution the more comfortable it is to work with. CAD software may also be used to display graphic elements in different colours for rendering purposes. High-resolution monochrome monitors display a single-colour black, white or green background.

Computer graphics: a general explanation _____

Pixel painting

The computer allows images to be drawn on a display screen by the lighting of a great number of small dots called *pixels*. Pixel graphics is the storing of an image as a grid of dots. Draughting and design are examples of vector graphics, another system in which a line is remembered by location, direction and length.

Modelling programs

These 3D programs are adaptable and, being flexible, are of more use to the design-oriented draughter. They are for modelling in 3D, from which 2D drawings can be extracted and in some cases sent to separate draughting programs, some of which might be graphics programs for rendering, presentations, and inclusion in documents.

Computer graphics in detail _____

Unlike drawing manually, which is an activity that requires a good eye to guide pen or pencil carefully across a set square or T-square, the computer-aided approach has several ways of producing drawings on a display screen.

There are two terms one must become familiar with at the outset: *commands* and *user interface*. When one draws with a computer, the user will operate a program by giving commands. The interface is what comes up on the screen and this generally tells the user what commands to give. There are various ways of communicating with the computer, as described below.

Typing in data

This method of inputting data is a way of producing computer-generated drawings on the monitor. The draughter uses the keyboard to type drawing notations and dimensions. The arrow keys can be used to move the screen cursor to create appropriate drawing shapes.

The keyboard method involves typing in English on a standard typewriter keyboard. This implies a knowledge of the necessary commands, which are often in single-letter codes. Typing skills are of the 'hunt and peck' method.

A menu enables commands to be chosen as a series of steps displayed on the screen. These are selected with a pointing device. A cursor or crosshairs then appear on the screen. The menu is sometimes placed to one side of the screen, taking up screen space and thus creating a smaller drawing area.

There are several pointing devices used with a menu; the following examples are the most widely used.

Electronic pencils

These come in several shapes and sizes. The function of the electronic pencil is to move the crosshairs around the screen. These 'pencils' often have a dual purpose: they point to on-screen graphics as well as choosing items from menus displayed on the screen. A *mouse* is a small box with buttons placed on the top and attached to the computer with a long tail flex. This device is moved around on a pad or desktop; this moves the crosshairs on the screen drawing the images that will develop finally into a complete drawing. A mouse is difficult to use at first, particularly for sketching, as it is awkward to move accurately and quickly.

Electronic mice comes in two types; *optical* and *mechanical*. The optical mouse has to be used on a pad which reflects a small light, while a mechanical mouse can be used on any flat surface. On earlier models a joystick was used, but this is a difficult way to draw lines onto the display screen.

The light pen

As the name implies, the light pen is held to the display screen either to select items from a menu or to draw with the crosshairs. This is the nearest approach to traditional drawing that the computer offers, although drawing with a light pen may result in a certain amount of eye strain, particularly on low-resolution and high-flicker video screens.

Digitizing

The mouse is a relative pointer: that is, it shows direction but it is not accurate at measuring distance. Because of this it cannot trace drawings. To do this, a digitizing tablet, which uses a button box (not a mouse) or an electronic stylus, is needed. The button box (also called a cursor) has a pair of crosshairs that trace over the drawing surface and is similar to the stylus.

Often the stylus is preferred as it is similar to a pencil. Tablet menus are also available and there are programs to create personal menus.

Using the voice

Speaking commands is an alternative to other methods of inputting data. Voice recognition systems comprise a microphone, an electronic board and special software that can translate the sound of the voice into tyepwritten script. This method of 'drawing' onto a screen by using the voice may be a way forward for the future of computer graphics and CAD.

The above interfaces are useful in their own ways. Draughters who have little experience often choose to put data into the computer by using a menu. On the other hand, some draughters prefer using a keyboard.

When entering data for use by the program it is important to recognize that coordinates can be input by marking a spot on the display screen with a pointing device or by typing in numbers (note that the CAD database file is mostly made up of coordinates). Entities already drawn may be selected in order to modify them by using a pointing device.

Most programs have the ability to include and display (but not include) other drawings within a drawing.

Programs are usually supplied with easy-to-read and understand

Fig. 6.2 A digitizing tablet.

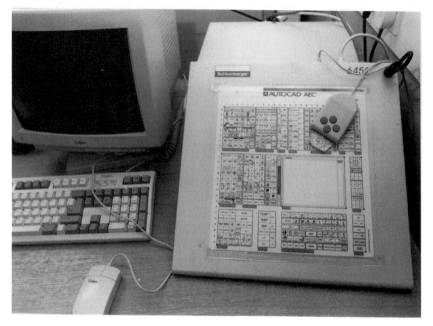

Fig. 6.3 A bit-pad and puck.

manuals, which are especially written to be 'user friendly'. However, these manuals can be very confusing to the person who is not used to working with a computer or sitting at a keyboard to produce drawings.

Printing and plotting

The drawing and draughting process that has been described relates to the electronic display on the video screen. To obtain what is called hard copy, there are several alternative methods to produce large, accurate and well-presented drawings very quickly.

There are two main methods: printing and plotting.

The quickest printing is done by a **laser printer**, either by an electrostatic process using a laser or LCD (liquid crystal diode) or an ink jet process. Another way is to print by an inkjet or an electronic laser. The process of converting the vector graphics on the display screen into a matrix of dots is called *rasterizing*.

Inkjet printers are generally used for text and graphics of medium resolution. This mode of printing does produce larger drawings of a reasonable quality.

Electrostatic printers have good resolution. They are accurate and fast. Architectural details and small drawings can be produced by desktop laser printers. Large printers for large drawings are very expensive and perhaps affordable only by printing agencies.

Pen plotters are superior to dot-matrix printers, and when they are working well, they produce a superior print in a relatively short time. The pen plotter works by moving a sheet of paper under a pen moving against the direction of the sheet. Another feature of a good pen plotter is its ability to use several pens at once and to provide different weights and colours of line. There are some disadvantages in that they can be rather noisy and sometimes the pens clog up; therefore constant supervision is essential.

The choice and cost of computer graphics

There are many proprietary computer graphics and CAD systems currently available at varying prices. The choice of the most appropriate system depends on the needs of the user. However, the software should be chosen with care before the user invests in expensive hardware. It is desirable to choose a system that is fast and easy to manipulate, otherwise there is no advantage over traditional methods of producing drawings. So far as the

Fig. 6.4　An inkjet printer.

Fig. 6.5   Hewlett Packard Draftpro DXL Pen Plotter (A1).

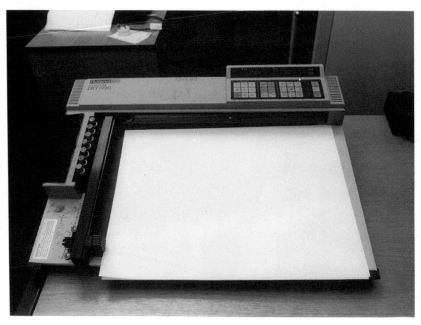

Fig 6.6   Rowland DXY 990 Flatbed Plotter (A3).

technical difficulties of learning the techniques necessary to use CAD effectively, the trend nowadays is towards user-friendly software that can be grasped very quickly by the user.

With printers/plotters, an important point to note is the size and cost of paper that each type of machine will handle. A4 laser printers are relatively cheap, but anything above A3 is quite expensive. Also for colour prints, A3-A0 pen or electrostatic plotters are also reasonable priced and inkjet printers are now available in A3. Generally speaking, inkjet printers are cheaper than lasers.

Finally it must be stressed that computer graphics and CAD have many advantages, particularly for large and expensive projects. In the future, exchanging CAD data between different CAD programs will become the norm. The computer may gradually become accepted for most projects, but traditional practice is being continually modified and a lengthy period of change and adjustment throughout the industry still lies ahead. Draughters must be aware of developments and be responsive to new ideas. The computer has undoubtedly created further opportunities as well as problems for architects, planners, engineers and others to develop their draughting, graphics, modelling and design skills. The drawing and design professions now have the choice of using computers to produce their drawings and designs or to use the more traditional approach as described in this book.

For the draughter/designer who is using CAD there is still a need to understand how drawings are actually put together.

Let us now look at a system that combines 2D draughting with 3D modelling. The ACROPOLIS system has been especially designed for architectural applications. The workstation in this system comprises four parts:

1. The graphics screen
2. The text screen to enable the operator to 'talk' to the system through typed commands and to receive instructions on how to proceed.
3. A keyboard, which enables the operator to type in alphabetic or numerical information.
4. A bit-pad and a device known as a puck, which is a hand-held pointing device with one or more buttons, to enable the operator to 'talk' to the system.

To get a line onto the screen the operator types in a command and presses the return key on the keyboard. The system prompts a vector which represents direction and distance and a further typed-in letter and return will bring a cursor (or crosshairs) onto the screen. When the puck is moved on the bit-pad the crosshairs/cursor will track around the screen. If the operator then presses the 'ON' button on the puck, an 'elastic' line will be generated; a further press of another button on the puck will fix the line on the screen.

Other buttons on the puck allow the operator to stop and start the sequence at will, leave gaps as required, move to a new location on the drawing or stop the sequence if necessary. Using this method a drawing shape, e.g. a rectangular plan shape, can be drawn quite rapidly.

Other ways of drawing straight lines in this program are by direction. The screen is split up into north, south, east and west and if a line is required up the screen, the operator types N and a distance (say 200 mm) and presses the return key. Similarly straight lines in the other directions can be made. This is a much more precise way of making lines of a measured length.

To outline the plan of a room, one can use a grid, which may be selected from the menu. The computer will then ask questions about the design tolerances of the room size to be drawn. After this has been established the operator can then generate the lines to draw the outline of the room, establishing door and window openings as required, using the crosshairs as described earlier.

When the outline of the room is completed, one can add fixtures and furniture by selecting predesigned symbols, such as windows and doors, from the menu on the bit-pad and position and angle them on the grid on the screen within the drawing. Similarly, the furniture can be selected from the menu and positioned and angled into place using the puck to guide the symbol on the screen. A wallfire, a settee, table, easy chairs, coffee table, TV etc. can all be pulled into the design from the menu on thie bit-pad in the same way. Each item can be moved around the screen to alter the angle to which it is set by simply positioning and pressing the appropriate button on the puck.

The room and furniture thus defined can now be made into an isometric projection by simply typing in ISOMETRIC selected from the menu. This can only be done in a 3D modelling system as opposed to the 2D system as the symbols are defined in the third dimension. In the PERSPECTIVE projection, the operator goes back into the 2D plan to indicate the 'eye height' required and the viewing position and focus of the viewer and to answer questions posed by the computer with regard as to whether a 60° normal or 80° wide-angle view is required.

The wall thickness and hatching can be achieved by first changing the menu sheet and selecting the appropriate symbols. The wall thickness is created by using corner unit symbols positioned on the plan and the wall lines stretched between them. Door and window opening symbols are put in on the plan afterwards.

Dimensions and other symbols can be put on in a similar way.

What normally happens in a design practice is that certain people are given specific tasks to do. Within the computer system these tasks, such as the drawing of external walls, windows, doors, furniture, pipework etc. become elemental layers, and this data is stored separately and then called up and combined into one drawing either on the screen or in the final plot in a sort of 'mix and match' process.

Computer drawings of elevations, sections, site plans etc. can be built up in a similar way by overlaying different types of drawing, one over the other, to form more complex drawings. Again, parts of previous drawings may be combined to form a completely new drawing. This selective copying and reusing is an important feature of CAD.

Finally, it must be remembered that the resulting seductive quality of the drawing plays an important part in selling the design, and one must be aware that the superb draughting quality may mask an indifferent design.

The above is a simplified description of just one system out of many on the market. Other systems have different methods of producing computer drawing: witness the example of a drawing of a summerhouse in Fig. 6.7. In this case a software package called AutoCAD was used. The titles were created by another packaged called Corel Draw, exported from a DXF file and imported into AutoCAD. A separate drawing was produced, which was attached to the principal drawing.

Fig. 6.7 Computer drawing of a summerhouse, Radstock (Barry Christian, Architect).

Fig 6.8 Computer generated plan of Brighton Hall Golf Club Clubhouse to show the possible quality of mechanical drawing. (Tony McCarthy)

7

Conventional Indications and Representation on Drawings

The following notes deal with various conventional methods of indicating details and representing materials on architectural drawings, with particular reference to production drawings.

Indication of dimensions

Traditional drawings

Reference has previously been made to the drawing of dimension lines. Fig. 7.1 shows portions of the plan, elevation and section of a building of solid construction, and illustrates how the dimension lines are arranged. Horizontal dimensions are shown on plan so far as possible. Generally, two lines are necessary, running parallel to and a short distance away from the outside walls. From every 'break' or change of direction of the wall and from every 'rough' opening in it, short perpendicular lines are taken to cut the inner dimension lines, and the dimensions of each horizontal part of the wall can then be figured between them. The outer dimension lines are used for the overall lengths of walls and are terminated by lines brought out at the ends of the building. Where the wall is long and divided up by pronounced breaks, these lengths may be indicated in addition to the overall length. Care must be taken that there is agreement between the inner and outer dimensions.

Dimension lines are also drawn inside the enclosing walls of the building 'a short distance from the inner faces. They are extended to cut the enclosing walls at right angles, and are dimensioned to show thicknesses of walls and partitions as well as lengths and widths of rooms between unfinished

SECOND FLOOR

window

FIRST FLOOR

floor level
broken line

window

GROUND FLOOR

PAVING

foundation

■ represents
dimension

SECTION

ELEVATION

PLAN

General principle of dimension lines

Fig. 7.1

column

column

B

A

PLAN   8

9 Framed building

Fig. 7.2

wall surfaces. It is usually impossible to put the dimension figures for wall thickness within the outlines of the walls, and they should therefore be put a little to one side with a link line to show to what they refer. Where it is necessary to show the height of a room on plan, the dimension should be enclosed in a circle.

Vertical dimensions are shown on section. Two vertical lines are drawn a little away from the outside walls, the inner one to show positions of openings in relation to floor levels and the outer one to show floor-to-floor heights. Sometimes a dimension line is put inside the building to show floor-to-ceiling heights or floor to inside sill heights, but generally this is not necessary. Overall heights, except where they have special meaning, are also unnecessary. Heights should not be taken from ground level, which is of course variable, but from some datum, usually a suitable point on the ground-floor level, although the required level of outside paving can be shown.

Horizontal broken lines should be drawn across elevations and sections at the various floor levels (see Fig. 7.1), and should be lettered: 'Basement', 'Ground Floor', 'First Floor', and so on. The floor levels can be shown at the ends of these lines in relation to a datum, those above the datum being prefixed by a + sign, and those below by a – sign, although if possible a suitable fixed point should be taken as job datum so that all other levels are positive. The figures should be enclosed in semicircles or rectangular 'boxes'. Levels should be given in metres to three decimal places, i.e. in millimetres. For large jobs it is usual to relate the job datum to the Ordnance Survey datum in the UK, or to an equivalent datum elsewhere. Exact positions of levels on plan should be marked by crosses, and the figures left unenclosed for existing levels or enclosed in 'boxes' or circles for intended levels.

In addition to the main dimension lines referred to above, other dimension lines may be necessary in order that the position of no part of the building is in doubt. All dimensions necessary for the carrying out of the work must be given. It should not be necessary to scale a drawing for this purpose other than a full-size detail. Dimensions that are not to scale, however, should be indicated by the addition of the letters 'NTS'.

Framed structures

Where the structure is framed, dimensions should be related to the column or stanchion centres, as shown in Fig. 7.2. This usually necessitates three outside dimension lines – the innermost one for 'breaks' and openings and stanchion centres, the middle one for stanchion centres only, and the outermost one for overall measurements – and the extension of column centre lines to reference numbers and letters. Centre lines in one direction are usually marked 1, 2, 3, etc. and in the other direction, A, B. C, etc., starting from the top left corner of the drawing. The system is applicable to both regular and irregular plan shapes, and the framing lines do not necessarily have to be straight or at right-angles to one another. Columns can be described by reference to the intersection of lines, e.g. B3 at the intersection of lines B and 3. Fig. 7.3 illustrates the basic principle.

Fig. 7.3

STRUCTURAL
STEELWORK

Representation of materials

Fig. 7.4 shows the conventional line indications of materials in general use.[1] All diagonal lines are at 45°. The spacing of the lines should be varied, of course, according to the scale of the drawing, but the general proportions shown here should be adhered to. A common error is to space the hatching for brickwork either too widely apart or too close together. Modifications according to the scale are suggested in regard to certain indications. Where large areas of hatching need to be indicated, and especially for such materials as plaster and concrete, only a portion near the edge or ends should be shown, the hatching gradually 'fading' towards the middle, as shown in the examples.

The elevational indications are for materials that are otherwise difficult to distinguish. The indication for glass should not be used for windows.

Where confusion is likely to occur in the interpretation of the indications a legend or key should be added to the drawing.

Indication of materials by colour is less used than formerly, but Table 7.1 gives a list recommended for standard practice.

[1]Reference should also be made to the current British Standard BS 1192, Part 3 1987.

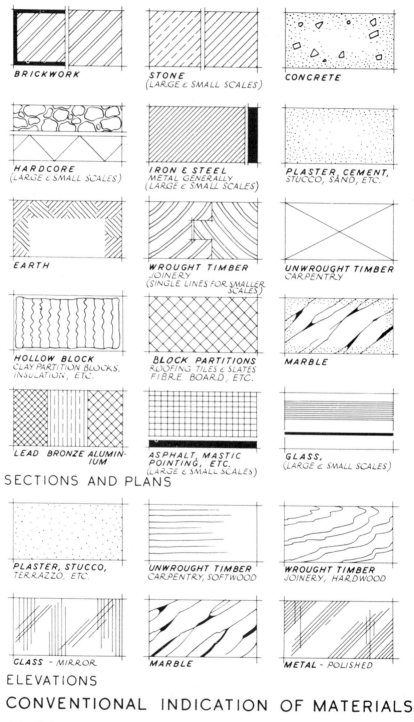

BRICKWORK

STONE
(*LARGE & SMALL SCALES*)

CONCRETE

HARDCORE
(*LARGE & SMALL SCALES*)

IRON & STEEL
METAL GENERALLY
(*LARGE & SMALL SCALES*)

PLASTER, CEMENT,
STUCCO, SAND, ETC.

EARTH

WROUGHT TIMBER
JOINERY
(*SINGLE LINES FOR SMALLER SCALES*)

UNWROUGHT TIMBER
CARPENTRY

HOLLOW BLOCK
CLAY PARTITION BLOCKS,
INSULATION, ETC.

BLOCK PARTITIONS
ROOFING TILES & SLATES
FIBRE BOARD, ETC.

MARBLE

**LEAD   BRONZE   ALUMIN-
IUM**

ASPHALT, MASTIC
POINTING, ETC.
(*LARGE & SMALL SCALES*)

GLASS,
(*LARGE & SMALL SCALES*)

SECTIONS AND PLANS

PLASTER, STUCCO,
TERRAZZO, ETC.

UNWROUGHT TIMBER
CARPENTRY, SOFTWOOD

WROUGHT TIMBER
JOINERY, HARDWOOD

GLASS - MIRROR

MARBLE

METAL - POLISHED

ELEVATIONS

CONVENTIONAL INDICATION OF MATERIALS

Fig. 7.4

For elevations, colouring should be in lighter washes of the specified colours for working drawings, but reasonable liberties are permissible to avoid a garish effect so long as misinterpretations are not likely to arise.

Colours and coloured lines should not, of course, be used on tracings or drawings from which photoprint reproductions may be required, but may in some cases be replaced by transferred mechanical tone.

Table 7.1 Recommended colours for representation of materials

Material	*Colour*	*Material*	*Colour*
Brick	Vermilion	Cast iron	Payne's grey
Concrete	Hooker,s green No. 1	Wrought iron	Prussian blue
Earth	Sepia	Granite, marble other natural stones	Cobalt blue
Hardcore or dry fill	Chrome yellow medium	Steel	Purple
Plaster	Terra verde	Cast or recon- structed stone	Viridian
Special plaster, acoustic, fibrous etc.	Mauve	Unwrought timber	Raw sienna
Asbestos cement	Neutral tint	Wrought timber	Burnt sienna (Vandyke brown for
Faience, tiles, etc.	Chrome orange		hardwood if to be distin- guished from softwood)
Cement screed	Payne's grey	Glass	Pale blue wash

Other materials at the discretion of the draughter.

Abbreviations

The following is a list of abbreviations of words commonly used on drawings. The list includes Imperial units which will eventually become obsolete, but are still likely to be seen on some drawings.

Primary units

Centimetre	cm	Cubic millimetre	mm3
Chain	ch.	Cubic yard	yd3 *or* cu yd
Cubic centimetre	cm3	Dozen	doz.
Cubic foot	ft3 *or* cu ft	Gramme	g
Cubic inch	in3 *or* cu in	Hundredweight	cwt
Cubic metre	m3	Inch	in

Kilogramme	kg	Square metre	m2
Metre	m	Square millimetre	mm2
Millimetre	mm	Square yard	yd2 *or* sq yd
Ounce	oz	Ton	ton
Pound	lb	Tonne	t
Square centimetre	cm2	Volt	V
Square foot	ft2 *or* sq ft	Yard	yd
Square inch	in2 *or* sq in		

Materials and general terms

Aggregate	Agg.	Ground level	GL
Air brick	AB	Gully	G
Approved	appd	Height	ht
Approximate	approx.	Hose bib	HB
Asbestos	Asb.	Inspection chamber	IC
Asphalt	Asph.	Insulated or insulation	insul.
Bench mark	BM	Intercepting trap	IT
Birmingham gauge	BG	Internal	int.
Bitumen	Bitn	Invert	inv.
Brickwork	Bwk *or* B	Lavatory basin	LB
British Standard	BS	Left hand	LH
Cast iron	CI	Macadam	Mac.
Cement	Cem.	Manhole	MH
Centre line	CL *or* C	Mild steel	MS
Centre to centre	c/c	Not to scale	NTS
Checked	ckd	Number	No.
Chemical closet	CC	Petrol interceptor	PI
Clearing eye	CE	Radius	rad.
Concrete	Conc.	Rainwater pipe	RWP
Corrugated	Corr.	Reinforced concrete	RC
Diameter	dia.	Right hand	RH
Drawing	Dwg	Rising main	RM
Drinking fountsin	DF	Rainwater outlet	RWO
Earth closet	EC	Round	rd
Figure	Fig.	Sink waste	SW
Fire hydrant	FH	Sink	S
Flushing cistern	FC	Sketch	sk.
Fresh air inlet	FAI	Sluice or stop valve	SV
Galvanized	Galv.	Soil and vent pipe	S&VP
Glazed-ware pipe	GWP	Soil pipe	SP
Grease trap	GT	Specification	Spec.

Spigot and socket	S&S	Vent pipe	VP
Square	sq.	Volume	vol.
Standard wire gauge	SWG	Waste pipe	WP
Stand pipe	St. P	Waste and vent pipe	W&VP
Street gully	SG	Water closet	WC
Tongued and grooved	T&G	Weight	Wt
Traced	Tcd	Yard gully	YG
Urinal	U		

Drawing and indication of constructional materials _

Brickwork

On plan and section indicated by solid black at small scales and by conventional hatching at 1:100 scale and upwards (although some consider 1:100 scale too small for hatching). On detail drawings the horizontal course lines are sometimes shown in addition to or instead of hatching on section, especially where there is some particular relevance to the construction. Difficulties occur with hatching on curved walls on plan, but there seems to be no solution to the problem, nor to the optical illusions that the diagonal lines of the hatching tend to produce. The worst effects, however, can be avoided by carefully considering the placing of the lines.

Fig. 7.5 shows the indication of brickwork on elevation at various scales. It is better to set out the heights of the courses on a vertical line at the left-hand side of the sheet and to rule across from this with the T-square than to set out the courses actually on the elevation, where the markings tend to become confused and are difficult to rub out. The courses can also be numbered and provide a means of checking other settings-out.

The courses are not usually shown at less than 1:100 scale, except in pencil on some careful design drawings. At 1:100 scale single lines are shown, individual bricks being indicated only for flat arches and similar features. At 1:50 scale vertical joints can be indicated also if necessary, but are not essential. At 1:20 scale and larger it is possible to show double lines to indicate the thicknesses of joints. In general, joint lines should be thinner than outlines whether in ink or pencil. They should extend over the whole area of the material or be confined to regular areas which will be sufficient to convey the required impression. The indication should not be spotted about the elevation, so camouflaging it and making it look in bad repair.

Figs. 7.6–7.8 show typical methods of setting out flat and segmental gauged arches and segmental rough arch in brickwork. The marking-out of the positions of the bricks and the finding of centres can be seen from the drawings, which are reproduced at approx. 1:20.

Masonry

Stone walls are indicated on plan and section solid black under 1:100 scale and sometimes at 1:100 scale, otherwise by conventional hatching. The courses are shown to the larger scales on section, and sometimes the individual stones are shown on plan, e.g. when the facing differs from the backing.

Rubble walling is shown on plan and section as more or less irregular. stones either in black with white joints or in outline. Fig. 7.9 shows plans and sections of three types of rubble walling at approximately 1:20 scale and the methods of drawing the corresponding elevations. It is important with masonry indication of this kind that the size, shape and arrangement of the stones are reasonably like the actual construction. Haphazard scribble will not do to indicate rubble, nor will careful drawing if long vertical joints occur and the stones at angles and openings are impossible in practice.

Fig. 7.10 shows part elevation of an ashlar masonry wall. Here the joints are or should be an integral part of the design and must be accurately shown. If the drawing is to give full information to the masons, the dimensions of every stone must be apparent and the stones may have to be numbered. The heights of the courses are usually taken from bed to bed of the joints and are shown on a vertical dimension line. Horizontal dimensions are shown on horizontal dimension lines passing through typical courses. Some additional dimension lines may be necessary around openings or similar features where the arrangement of the stones is varied. Openings must be dimensioned. Plans and sections give the third dimensions of the stones.

Stones are crossed – diagonal lines from corner to corner – on elevation where otherwise their shape and size might not be clear owing to dimension or other lines. It is generally unnecessary to cross every stone.

There seem to be various methods of numbering the stones, but the logical system is to follow more or less the sequence in which they are laid. Each course is indexed by letters referring to the approximate orientation of the elevation on which it occurs and its position in relation to other courses. In the example illustrated the distinguishing letters are: S for south elevation and A, B, C, etc., for the sequence of cources starting at the bottom. If the alphabet becomes exhausted, then it begins again doubled, AA, BB, CC, although some abbreviation is necessary if the building is of considerable height. The stones take the indexing of their course and are numbered from left to right. Note that where there is a return elevation the stones that appear on two elevations take their numbers from the elevation on which the larger faces show. No stone can have two numbers. The numbers are put in the top left-hand corners of the stones on the drawing.

SCALE 1:100

SCALE 1:50

SCALE 1:20

BRICKWORK IN ELEVATION

Fig. 7.5

⅛ WIDTH OF OPENING

DIVISIONS

SETTING OUT OF FLAT
GAUGED "ARCH"

Fig. 7.6

DIVISIONS

RISE

SETTING OUT OF GAUGED
BRICK ARCH

Fig. 7.7

DIVISIONS

RISE

SETTING OUT OF ROUGH
BRICK ARCH

Fig. 7.8

SECTION | ELEVATION

STONES DRAWN SEPARATELY
FREEHAND

**RANDOM
RUBBLE**

PLAN

SILL

SECTION | ELEVATION

JOINTS DRAWN IN
FREEHAND

SETTING OUT
LINES RULED

**COURSED
RUBBLE**

PLAN

RUBBLE
BACKING

LINTOL

JOINTS RULED

SECTION | ELEVATION

**SNECKED
RUBBLE**

PLAN

Fig. 7.9

PART ELEVATION OF ASHLAR WALL
TO SHOW DIMENSIONING, NUMBERING OF STONES, ETC.

MASONRY

Fig. 7.10

Timber

On plan and section timber-frame construction is shown either as a solid black wall of appropriate thickness at small scales or in outline with solid black studs or framing. At 1:50 scale and larger it is possible to show the outer and inner facings and cross the studs, etc., in the conventional manner for unwrought timber. Fig. 7.11 shows part plan, section and elevation of a small timber building.

On elevation, continuous thin lines are drawn to represent vertical or horizontal boarding as the case may be. Cross joints are not usually shown. Edges that are intentionally irregular can be drawn freehand over ruled construction lines.

Steelwork

Fig. 7.12 shows the drawing and conventional indication of typical details and sections of structural steelwork.

Steel sections when adjacent and shown solid black to a small scale should have a thin white space – the thickness of a line – left between them.

Fig. 7.13 shows part of a steel-framing plan, the type of drawing, usually at 1:1 scale, prepared to show details of the beams at each floor level for a steel-framed building. The conventional indication for such a plan is shown in Fig. 7.14. Fig. 7.3 shows an alternative method of annotating the grid lines of a steel-framed building.

Note that steelwork on, say, the third-floor framing plan is the steel carrying the third floor, and the stanchions are the ones running from second to third floor.

A typical column or stanchion schedule, sometimes shown on the drawings, is also shown in Fig. 7.14. Stanchions usually run through two floors and are spliced a short distance above floor level.

When the drawings of a building are to be used by a structural engineer, who sometimes prepares the framing plan as a tracing over the architect's drawings, they should show: the nature and thicknesses of all walls; the nature and thickness or the weights of all floor finishes; maximum possible depths for all beams; positions and weights of any heavy loads, such as tanks, machinery and lifts.

Reinforced concrete

Fig. 7.15 shows related details of various kinds and at various scales to show the drawing of reinforced concrete construction for general indications.

RIDGE

SHINGLE ROOFING
(DRAWN FREEHAND OVER RULED LINES)

RAFTERS

CEILING JOISTS

HEAD

DOUBLE BEAM

GUTTER
FASCIA &
SOFFIT

MITRED CORNER

ANGLE
STUDS

INTERNAL
PARTITION

EXTERNAL
WALL

STANDARD
WOOD WINDOW

CORNER BOARDS

PLANS

FLASHING

PLASTER OR OTHER
INTERNAL FINISH

STUDS

PLAN

DIAGONAL
SHEATHING

WEATHER-
BOARDING

SOLE PLATE
FLOORING

SUB FLOOR

HEADER
JOISTS

PLATE
D.P.C.
W.I. ANCHORS

AIR BRICK

SURFACE
CONCRETE

HARDCORE

ELEVATION

BASE WALL

FOUNDATION

SCALE 1:50

SECTION   *Fig. 7.11*

Representation and plan indication of details and fittings

Doors

Fig. 7.16 shows an example of the drawing of a door and frame at various scales. This indicates the amount of detail that can be reasonably included in each case. It is a common mistake to attempt to show too much at the smaller scales. No hard and fast rules can be laid down, however, and it may be permissible to show more in a carefully executed design drawing than in a working drawing. Fig. 7.17 shows typical conventional plan indications of doors at small scale. The door is indicated by a single line at right angles to the wall and the swing of its opening edge by a quadrant or semi circle. Note that the centre of the arc must be where the pin of the hinge is. Where the door lines at right angles to the wall might be confused with other lines on the drawing, they can be shown at a lesser angle provided the indication is consistent throughout the drawing. An alternative indication is the use of a straight line at 45° instead of the quadrant curve. This method saves time as such lines can be drawn by pen or pencil and set square quicker and easier than can curves by compasses. However, it is less expressive and can cause confusion to those unfamiliar with the convention.

Windows

Wood windows

Fig. 7.18 shows an example of the drawing of a typical wood casement window at various scales. Double-hung sashes should be denoted at small scales by the letters 'DHS' on plan and elevation.

Metal windows

Fig. 7.19 shows the representation at various scales of a typical metal window. Note particularly the indication of the metal sections, which cannot be drawn satisfactorily in full at less than 1:10. As metal windows are standard products they are not usually detailed except in relation to other construction, and the indication of the opening parts in elevation is therefore all the more necessary. It used to be the general practice to cross the opening parts, but the conventional indication shown in Fig. 7.20, which denotes the hinged side or pivot of the opening, is becoming general.

ELEVATIONS

HALF FULL-SIZE

PLANS

RIVET   BOLT   WELD

ELEVATIONS

PLANS

RIVET BOLT WELD
INDICATION AT SMALL SCALES

CHANNEL
HALF FULL-SIZE

INDICATION AT SMALL SCALES

Fig. 7.12

ELEVATION

PLAN

SECTION

DETAIL OF TYPICAL
JOINTING OF BEAM
AND STANCHION
INDICATION AT SMALL SCALES

ISOMETRIC

S T E E L W O R K

PART OF STEEL FRAMING PLAN   *Fig. 7.13*

STANCHIONS

PLATED STANCHIONS

STANCHION Nos.

BEAMS

PLATED BEAMS   P. B.

BEAM NUMBERS   A(123)
  AND SIZES   12"x 5" I 32

STRUTS

ECCENTRICITIES |4"   4"|

BEAM REACTIONS   5·0   3·6

CRANKED BEAMS

WIND BRACING

CONVENTIONAL
INDICATIONS FOR
PLANS

STRUCTURAL
STEELWORK
IMPERIAL DIMENSIONS

PART OF TYPICAL
COLUMN SCHEDULE *Fig. 7.14*

DETAIL OF SLAB

DISTRIBUTING RODS
RODS
d

MAIN BEAM
PILLAR
SECONDARY BEAMS
FOUNDATION
MAIN BEAM
PILLAR

KEY PLAN

a
b
c
d
e
f

MAIN BEAM BAR DIAGRAM *HALF SCALE OF DETAIL.*

SECTION THRO'
MAIN BEAM AT
MID-SPAN.
MAIN BEAM
SLAB
SECONDARY
BEAM
HAUNCH
f a b c d e

NOT LESS
THAN 4D
4D +
D
DETAIL OF BENT-UP
END OF BAR

PILLAR

PILLAR

SECONDARY
BEAM
MAIN
BEAM
SLAB
PILLAR

AXONOMETRIC
DETAIL OF
PILLAR, BEAMS
AND SLAB.

PLAN OF
FOUNDATION

DETAIL OF TYPICAL
FOUNDATION, PILLAR
AND MAIN BEAM

R E I N F O R C E D
C O N C R E T E   *Fig. 7.15*

Domestic kitchen equipment

Fig. 7.21 shows the conventional indication on plan and elevation at 1:100 scale of various equipment and fittings.

Sanitary fittings

Fig. 7.22 shows the conventional indication on plan and elevation at 1:100 scale of various sanitary fittings. The centres of arcs are shown in some cases, although these would not appear in the drawing. Alternatives are given in the cases of baths, bidets, and WCs. Clear plastic templates are available for drawing these and other symbols.

Furniture, etc.

Fig. 7.23 shows a common conventional indications of domestic furniture at 1:100 scale. These articles, with the possible exception of beds, are not shown on working drawings unless forming parts of the permanent structure. If known, the sizes can be made to conform to those of the articles to be used, but this is not always the case when 1:100 scale drawings are being prepared. To larger scales more precise details of the equipment would be given.

Staircases, etc.

Fig. 7.24 shows the setting-out and indication of various types of staircases. The easiest way of dividing up the floor-to-floor height into the required number of risers or the length of the flight into treads is by using the edge of a scale on the drawing in the manner described on page 36. Arrows should be used to indicate the 'UP' direction only. The putting of arrows pointing in both directions and labelling them 'up' and 'dn' respectively is a waste of time and leads to confusion. The first riser can be indicated on the line of the arrow by a dot. All risers should be numbered in order, beginning with the lowest, on production drawings, both on plan and section.

Lifts are indicated as shown, the car usually being crossed.

Ramps should be labelled and have an arrow pointing in the 'up' direction. The angle of rise – 15° maximum – should be given on section.

LINTOL

VENEER

BEAD

GLASS

GLAZED PANEL

LEVER HANDLE

1:10   1:200

VENEERED SURFACE

ARCHITRAVE

1:50

1:20

REPRESENTATIONS AT VARIOUS SCALES

large scale details

D O O R   *Fig. 7.16*

ARCS CONTINUED TO INDICATE DOORS TO FASTEN

alternative indications

SINGLE FOLDING   DOUBLE FOLDING   SWING   REVOLVING

SLIDING (RECESS)   SLIDING (FACE)   FOLDING & SLIDING (END HUNG)

PLAN INDICATION OF DOORS

Fig. 7.17

TOP-HUNG
FANLIGHT

SIDE-HUNG
CASEMENT

1:100   1:100

1:20   1:50

PLANS ELEVATIONS
AND SECTIONS

Fig. 7.18

R.C. LINTOL

HEAD

STEEL
BUTT

TRANSOM

SASH
HEAD

PUTTY

GLAZING

BOTTOM
RAIL

SASH
HEAD

large scale
details

MULLION   JAMB

BOTTOM
RAIL

CILL

STEEL
BUTT

WOOD WINDOW

REPRESENTATIONS AT VARIOUS SCALES

1:100   1:200

1:50

1:20

PLANS, ELEVATIONS AND SECTIONS

TOP HUNG FANLIGHT

SIDE HINGED CASEMENT

GLAZING BARS

HEAD

POINTING

PUTTY

GLAZING

TRANSOM
(as Mfrs' details)

GLAZING BAR

FRAME

POINTING   CILL

large scale details

TOP HINGED   BOTTOM HINGED   HORIZONTAL PIVOTTED

L.H. SIDE HINGED   VERTICAL PIVOTTED
R.H. SIDE HINGED   HORIZONTAL TOP PIVOTTED

L   R   L   R

SLIDING   FOLDING & SLIDING

CONVENTIONAL INDICATION OF OPENING LIGHTS

Fig. 7.20

GLAZING BAR

MULLION
(as Mfrs' details)   FRAME   JAMB

Fig. 7.19

METAL WINDOW

REPRESENTATIONS AT VARIOUS SCALES

SECT.   ELEVATION   SECT.   SECT. ELEVATIONS   SECT.

STANDARD CUPBOARDS   SINKS

WOOD,
STEEL OR
PLASTICS

SEPARATE
DRAINER

WIDTHS VARY
PLANS

METAL OR PORCELAIN ENAMEL
SINGLE OR DOUBLE DRAINERS
VARIOUS SIZES.

LAUNDRY
TUB

L.T.

SIDE : ELEVATIONS   SIDE : ELEVATIONS   ELEVATIONS

COOKERS   REFRIGERATOR   DISH   WASH   H.W.
                                        WASHER BOILER BOILER

C   GAS OR ELECTRIC   SOLID FUEL   R   UNDER COUNTER   W.B.
     AVERAGE SIZES   TYPE   AVE.DOMESTIC
PLANS   SIZE

CONVENTIONAL INDICATION OF EQUIPMENT

1:100

DUCT   SINK

REFRIG.
UNDER

COOKER

KITCHEN

CUP'DS   TABLE

BROOMS

DINING ROOM

PLAN

TYPICAL EXAMPLE OF   AXONOMETRIC
KITCHEN OF SMALL HOUSE

DOMESTIC KITCHENS   *Fig. 7.21*

SHOWER HEAD

SHOWER
CURTAIN RAIL

MIRROR

SHELF

CURTAIN

IF WITH
PEDESTAL

SECTIONS   SECTION   ELEVATION SECT.

BATHS   SHOWER BASIN

LOW LEVEL
CISTERN

ELEVATION   ELEVATIONS

BIDET   W.C.

ALTERNATIVE
INDICATION
OF PLAN

PLANS

CORNER
LAVATORY BASIN

**CONVENTIONAL
INDICATION OF
FITTINGS**

1:100

SECT.   ELEVATION   ELEVATION

URINALS   TOWEL
RAIL

T.U.   S.U.
TROUGH URINAL SLAB URINAL

STALLS

WALL AND
CORNER
HUNG URINALS

PLANS

TOWEL
RAIL

BASIN

BATH

BATHRM.   W.C.

SHOWER

PLAN

**TYPICAL EXAMPLE
OF BATHROOM AND W.C.**

AXONOMETRIC

SANITARY FITTINGS   *Fig. 7.22*

Graphic symbols

Electric symbols

Fig. 7.25 shows the symbols used in connection with interior electrical installations. These and other symbols are contained in British Standard Specification BS 1192 Part 3 1987.

Plumbing, drainage, etc

Fig. 7.26 shows some of the symbols and ways of indicating pipe runs and details in connection with plumbing and drainage plans and drawings to show gas, water, heating and ventilation layouts, etc.

Complete lists of symbols can be obtained from the appropriate engineering institutions.

Examples of drawings for small house

Figs. 7.27–7.29 illustrate typical traditional-type production drawings for an economical four-bedroom house. The layout of the sheet was suggested in Fig. 5.12. The ground floor plan and the north-east elevation are reproduced at approximately 1:100 scale.

The manner of dimensioning and lettering the drawings and the conventional indications have been previously referred to. Note the use of arrows to indicate entrances. It is usual to describe floor finishes of each room on plan; this is done by smaller lettering under the names of the rooms.

Alterations and additions

Fig. 7.30 shows typical examples of the indication and suitable notes for use on drawings showing alterations or additions to existing buildings. The existing and proposed work must be clearly distinguished. Usually only the minimum essential outlines of the former are drawn (see 'junction'), the new work being indicated in the normal manner. Existing walls are usually outlined in a heavy black line or blacked in solid. When drawings are coloured the colouring is confined to the new work.

Full-size details

These are drawings to show details of construction or, less often, designs that cannot be shown sufficiently clearly on small-scale drawings for the set-

SECTION ELEVATIONS ELEVATIONS SECT.

SETTEE   CHAIR   PIANOS

CHAIR

STOOL

PLANS

LIVING   ROOM

SECT. ELEVATION SECT. ELEV. ELEVATION ELEVATION

SIDEBOARD   CHAIR   DINING TABLES

BENCH

ALTERNATIVE INDICATION

PLANS

DINING   ROOM

SIDE ELEVATIONS ELEVATIONS SIDE ELEVATION

WARDROBE   BEDS

PLANS

BEDROOM

SINGLE DOUBLE

INDICATION OF CARPET, CORKSHEET, LINO, OR OTHER UNPATTERNED FLOOR COVERING

FOR VINYL AND CORK TILES, ETC SHOW SQUARES

ALTERNATIVE INDICATION SHOWN BY BROKEN LINES

FURNITURE   1:100

Fig. 7.23

STAIR WELL

14 13 12 11 10 9 8 7 6 5 4 3 2 1

HEADROOM

EDGE OF SCALE

SECTION   ELEVATION

TOTAL RISE

SECTION   ELEVATION

BROKEN LINES TO INDICATE HIDDEN STEPS

14 13 12 11 10 9 8 7 6 5 4 3 2 1

LANDING

ARROWS ON PLAN POINT UPWARDS

TOTAL GOING

EDGE OF SCALE

PLAN

STRAIGHT   FLIGHT

BROKEN LINES TO INDICATE STEPS ABOVE PLAN LEVEL

RISERS NUMBERED BEGINNING WITH LOWEST

8 9   7 6 5 4 3 2 1

PLAN

DOG-LEGGED   STAIRS

LINES OF HANDRAILS

ELEVATION   ELEVATION

STOREY ROD

14 13 12 11 10 9 8 7 6 5 4 3 2 1

DETAIL OF STEP

PLAN

SPIRAL STAIR

WALKING LINE

3-CENTRE ELLIPSE CONSTRUCTION

PLAN

ELLIPTICAL STAIR

45°

CAR INDICATED BY CROSSED RECTANGLE TO SMALL SCALE

PLAN   **LIFT**

15° MAX.

ANGLE OF RISE

ELEVATION

RAMP UP

PLAN

RAMP

S T A I R S   E T C.   INDICATION AND SETTING OUT

Fig. 7.24

Power outlets

Socket outlet, to BS 1363, any type

Socket outlet, to BS 1363, two gang

Socket outlet, to BS 4343, with indicating lamp

Socket outlet, to BS 4343, with two pole switch

Switches

One pole, one way

One pole, two way

One pole, intermediate

Two pole, one way

Three pole, one way

Four pole, one way

Socket, FM radio

Socket, public service television

Socket, private service television

Socket, closed circuit television

Communications sockets

Public service television — TV

Private service television — PTV

Closed circuit television — CCTV

Telephone — T

Manholes and gullies

Gully, any type

Horizontal inlet gulley

Vertical inlet gulley

Rectangular manhole

Circular manhole

Rectangular back drop manhole

Circular backdrop manhole

Sealed invert access plate

Petrol/oil/grease separator

Push button, any type

Supply and distribution

Main intake board

Distribution board

Isolator

Electricity meter

Terminal to be connected to earth

Fuse

Circuit breaker

Lightning protection

Air handling equipment

Centrifugal fan

Fan, any type

Fig. 7.25   These sysmbols are based on BS 1192 Part 3: 1987.

Windows in elevation

Perimeter outline		'Slide and tilt'	
Hinge (pivot) axis		'Slide and tilt' showing secondary function	
Pivot point		'Tilt and turn'	
Slide to open		'Tilt and turn' showing secondary function	
Reversible		Fixed	F
Fixed (not openable)	F	Hinged at side	
Secondary function	- - -	Hinged at bottom	
Any type		Pivotted, horizontal axis	
Moving axis, hinged, vertical axis		Pivotted, horizontal axis, reversible	
Moving axis, hinged, horizontal axis		Pivotted, vertical axis	
Sliding horizontally		Pivotted, vertical axis, asymmetrical	
Sliding vertically		Pivotted, vertical axis, reversible	

Luminaires

Spot/projector, any type	
Spot/projector, enclosed	

Fig. 7.26   These sysmbols are based on BS 1192 Part 3: 1987.

ting-out of workshop drawings. They are usually made for carpenters', join-ers' and masons' work. They are drawn on tracing or detail paper and are largely sectional in type. All members are shown to exact finished shape and size.

The drawing is made in strong pencil line or ink and the sections of each member may be outlined with coloured pencils or pens or by a band of water-colour in the conventional colours. Lengthy sections are often divided up for convenience, although sometimes they are drawn on a con-tinuous roll of paper.

Workshop drawings

These further working drawings, nearly always to full size, are usually made by foremen or special 'setters-out' in the workshops of the various trades, etc., from the architect's scale drawings and full-size details. Sometimes, however, architects prefer to make the workshop drawings themselves.

From these workship drawings the working lines are transferred to the material or templates. They are made on thick cartridge paper or on spe-cially prepared boards of straight-grained timber or sheets of plywood about 2.5 m long. The boards are termed 'rod'. Their surfaces are glass-papered and covered with a thin coating of whitewash and size or are chalked over, and the drawing is done with a strong pencil line. Coloured pencils are sometimes used to emphasize sections.

Fig. 7.31 shows two setting-out rods, one for a four-panelled door, the other for a cupboard with sliding door. The boards bear job numbers, and sometimes the various members of the work are given reference numbers.

Checklist for operational drawings

The following refers to some of the main points to be dealt with in making traditional operational drawings. All of them may not apply to every job, and other items can be added to the list according to individual ideas. Such a list does, however, help to avoid omissions.

General

1. Careful arrangements of sheets and drawings for maximum legibility and help to users.
2. Use of standard signs, hatching and symbols.
3. Compliance with Building Regulations, planning authorities' requi-ments, etc.

Fig. 7.27

Fig. 7.28

NORTH-EAST ELEVATION *Fig. 7.29*

SCALE 1:100

ALTERATIONS AND ADDITIONS
TYPICAL EXAMPLES OF INDICATION

Fig. 7.30

4. Dimension lines and dimensions. agreement of total lengths, etc.
5. All necessary notes, labelling, titles, north-point, scale, etc.
6. Indication of entrances.
7. Direction of stairs, numbering of risers.
8. Numbering of doors, windows and other plan units.
9. Door swings.
10. Floor finishes.
11. Direction of ramps.
12. Sanitary fittings. Only fittings made or ordered by contractor to be shown.
13. Positions of artificial light points, etc.
14. Positions of radiators.
15. Positions of service points.
16. Levels in relation to ordnance or other data.

Basement plan

1. Foundations of structural walls.
2. Steppings in site and foundation concrete.
3. Tanking.
4. Casing of steelwork, numbering of stanchions, etc.
5. Thickness of heating chamber wails, fireclay lining to flues.
6. Positions of boilers, etc.
7. Finished level of heating chamber floor and surface concrete.
8. Electrical intake and switch room.
9. Boiler room sump.
10. Drainage of areas.
11. Ducts for pipes.
12. Gullies.
13. Drainage pipe lines,. manholes, invert levels and arrows to show direction of fall, interceptor and f.a.i.

Ground and upper floors

1. Site layout.
2. Numbering of stanchions, etc., steel beams, sizes, weights, levels.
3. Sleeper walls dotted.
4. Directions of floor spans.
5. Ducts; flues.
6. Drainage lines, manholes, etc.; rainwater, soil, vent pipes, etc.
7. Fuel chute.
8. Railings to areas.

Fig. 7.31

SETTING-OUT RODS

4-PANELLED DOOR
SETTING-OUT ROD

SLIDING DOOR CUPBOARD
SETTING·OUT ROD

Roof plan

1. Direction of falls.
2. Positions of rainwater pipes, vent pipes, etc., cesspools, rainwater heads.
3. Tanks and circulation.
4. Stacks.
5. Type of covering.
6. Directions of spans.
7. Access to roof.

Elevations and sections

1. Levels of floors, etc. in relation to data.
2. Dimensions of heights of windows, etc.
3. Joint lines.
4. Stonework blocks crossed where necessary.
5. Joints of all unit materials.
6. Types, numbers and openings of windows.
7. Exposed pipes, gullies, etc., to be shown.
8. Airbricks, to rooms and timber ground floors, etc.
9. Foundations and steepings – show by broken line on all elevations.
10. Steps, ramps, railings, etc.
11. Existing ground line, finished paving line.
12. DPCs; tanking.
13. Stacks.

8

Tracings and Reproduction of Drawings

Tracings are made for the purpose of copying or developing existing drawings, whether on drawing paper or tracing paper, and are used either as finished drawings in themselves or, more often, as negatives for reproduction by photoprinting.

Tracing media are briefly described in Chapter 1. Any appropriate drawing method can be used, but usually lines are drawn in pencil or in indian ink or a combination of both, e.g. plans, elevations, etc. in pencil with dimensions and lettering in ink. Transfer lettering, tones and figures can also be used. Pencil work is best carried out using a fairly hard lead – selected in accordance with prevailing humidity – of a type specially made to give a dense yet crisp line free from grittiness, dust and smearing. Firm, even pressure is needed, but not so great as to 'bite' into the paper, or any subsequent erasures may result in 'ghosting'.

Ink lines are best drawn using one of the drawing pens previously described, which overcome most of the inconsistencies of thickness, risks of smudging, and general inconvenience associated with the old-style ruling pen. Nevertheless, the beginner may have difficulty with wayward and ragged lines until practice perfects control. A piece of paper for trying out the pen and a lint-free cloth for keeping the nib or point clean should be handy. The general sequence of drawing should be as recommended for inking-in on page 29. Ink lines should be of thicknesses according to their purposes and should not be unduly fine or they may fail to be reproduced in the printing process. Main outlines can be thickened for clearer definition. In ink drawings, details that are not to be given prominence in the printing can be drawn in a hard pencil, e.g. brick courses, hatching or shading.

With all drawing on tracing media it is essential that the surface is worked over or touched by hand as little as possible. If not to be traced over an existing drawing or grid, the general arrangement should be pre-established and main lines should be set up on a preliminary sheet over which the final drawing is made. Unless the final drawing is to be completed in one operation, it is as well to divide it into sections to be completed in turn. This procedure will also minimize trouble arising from movement of the paper due to overnight stretching or shrinkage in conditions of variable humidity. Sections of the drawing not being worked on should always be kept covered by strips of tracing paper for protection.

Before using tracing paper, a large sheet should be allowed to adjust itself to the atmosphere where it is to be used; the material is affected by moisture in theair when taken straight from the roll or packet.

Care must be taken in making corrections on tracing media. If the surface is damaged, marks will show on the copies. Erasures can be made most easily on paper and cloth by means of a razor blade. Unwanted pencil lines and dirt can be removed by an eraser.

Finished drawings on tracing paper can be coloured by dry techniques.

Reproduction of drawings

The following are the main types of photocopying processes for making copies of drawings. Copies are usually referred to as 'prints'.

Photostats

This is a normal photographic process using a camera for making copies of any kind of drawing or document. It is a two-stage process. A true negative is first made, i.e. white lines on a black background, from which positive prints, of the same size as the original, or proportionately larger or smaller, can be made on a variety of papers as best suited to the subject. If prints are subsequently to be coloured they should have a matt surface. Copies on translucent materials can be made, thus enabling them to be reproduced by dyeline process without need for intermediate tracing.

Mention may be made here of the microfilming of drawings, a photographic process by which miniature transparencies are made for convenience of safe storage and retrieval. Also, there are various kinds of ordinary office copiers – thermographic, electrographic and diffusion transfer – which, although developed primarily for the copying of typed or printed documents, are excellent for the rapid copying of small drawings (or larger drawings in parts that can be subsequently joined). Larger models, up to A1 size, are capable of making master copies of drawings for reproduction by the dyeline process.

Photocopies

Drawings can now be copied easily on large photocopiers and plan printers, which have superseded the dyeline or diazo process, which produces 'same size' printing from drawings done on tracing paper and film.

The dyeline process was the placing, face up, of an original tracing, sometimes called the negative, on top of ultraviolet light-sensitive coated print paper. This was then fed into a machine exposing this print paper to a high-intensity UV light, through the translucent original tracing. Levels of contrast between the printed image and background were regulated by the speed control on the machine: the faster the speed, the darker the print and vice versa.

The second operation of the dyeline process involved separating the original from the exposed print and feeding the print through an ammonia vapour field, where the ammonia reacted with the unexposed coating of the paper to 'dye line' to give the black/blue line characteristic of the dyeline print process.

The modern copier is basically a photocopier, which dispenses with the use of light-sensitive paper and ammonia and prints drawings done on 80 gsm paper, 90/95 gsm tracing paper as well as drafting film.

A modern copier is operated by the following steps:

1. Document input can be selected according to the lightness or darkness of the document to be copied.
2. Fusing temperature can be selected for the type of copy output material being used i.e. paper, tracing paper, polyester and drafting film.
3. Copy contrast can be selected to produce copies that are darker or lighter than normal.
4. The number of copies required can be displayed on a counter.

Copies can be made to any reasonable length, but they must be at least 297 mm long, and from 210 mm to 914 mm wide. The output material is inserted first, centred on the paper feed tray, where it will stop and wait for the document to be copied.

The document to be copied is then inserted face down and centred on the document feed shelf. The document will begin to feed when the document is inserted. Both the copy paper and the document will exit from the copier together.

(a) A black and white photocopier.

Fig. 8.1   (b) A Cannon colour Laser copier 300.

9
Perspective Drawing

Perspective projection

Perspective drawings convey more or less the actual appearance of the building or object. and are therefore of considerable value in enabling the lay person to appreciate points of design that are not easily understood from orthographic projections. There are a number of ways of setting up perspectives, the underlying theories are complex, and can only be described in words at great length. The best way to learn to make perspectives, however, is to study the essential principles from examples and then to practise their application.

What is probably the most satisfactory method for general use is illustrated in Figs. 9.1–9.5. Fig. 9.1 shows in orthographic projection the plan and two adjacent elevations of a rectangular prism or block. and how it is set up in perspective to give a view such as would be obtained by looking obliquely at the block from a level slightly above it.

The first step is to draw the plan of the block. Then the position of 'eye' of the spectator, point S, in relation to the plan according to the view required must be decided. The position is a matter of judgement in the light of experience, but a little imagination will help the beginner to get it somewhere near where it is wanted. Assuming for simplification that the spectator is looking directly at the near corner of the block, a line is drawn from S through this corner. This line is the *direct line of vision*, and somewhere along its length another line to represent the *picture plane* is drawn at right angles. The picture plane is an imaginary vertical plane on to which is projected the required view: see axonometric diagram in Chapter 3. Through the remaining corners of the block on plan further lines are drawn from S to the picture plane to locate these points in the perspective. Lines are also drawn from S parallel to the sides of the block to the picture plane. These points, VP1 and VP2, locate the positions of the vanishing points along the eye-level to which, in the perspective, the outlines of the sides of the block will converge. Another line is also drawn on plan in continuation of one or other side of the block to the picture plane; this line – shown broken in the figure – gives a point on the picture for the position of a *height line*.

Elevations

Plan

ORTHOGRAPHIC
PROJECTION

PERSPECTIVE
PROJECTION

Fig. 9.1

PICTURE PLANE

DIAGRAM

The next step is to draw the 'elevation', as it were, of the picture plane, which, although shown bounded in the diagram, is actually not defined in extent. At some reasonable distance above the plan, therefore, a horizontal line is drawn; this line represents the *eye-level* of the spectator, and to it are projected perpendiculars from the picture plane on plan from VP1 and VP2 and the point for the height line. As the view required is one looking down on the block, then a point must be marked down the height line from the eye-level equal to the estimated position of the eye above the 'ground' or horizontal plane on which the block rests. Through this point a horizontal line is drawn, called the *ground line*. Up the height line from the ground line is measured the height of the block taken from the elevation, i.e. at the same scale as the plan of the block. Through the point obtained and from the intersection of ground line and height line, lines are drawn from VP 1 to contact the direct line of vision continued from the plan. From the points of contact lines are drawn to VP2, and then by projecting up from the picture plane on plan it will be seen how the outline of the block in perspective is obtained.

Fig. 9.2 shows the application of the same method to the making of a perspective of the small garage shown in orthographic projection in Fig. 5.2. Most of the construction lines are shown. In drawing the plan of the garage it is only necessary to show in detail the outside lines of the two sides that will appear in the perspective, but care must always be taken that every salient feature is indicated.

The direct line of vision should preferably not pass through the near corner of the building and never so as to bisect it or the effect will be spoiled. A good way of fixing its position is to draw lines from S to the limits of the building, or wider if it is proposed to include much of the surroundings in the picture; the angle formed by these lines, which is termed the *angle of vision* and which should be between 40° and 60° to correspond to the normal range, is then bisected to find the direct line of vision.

The picture plane must always be at right angles to the line of vision, and the angle between the lines drawn to locate the vanishing points must also be a right angle.

In the perspective of the garage the eye-level has been taken at a height of 1 m above ground level. 'Normal' eye-level can be regarded as about 1600 mm above ground level, but somewhat lower than this is better for small buildings.

Note that three height lines have been taken, one for wall heights and details in the same planes, one for the eaves, and one for the ridge. As many height lines as convenient may be taken for the location of such features as chimney stacks and dormers, but the fewer the better. With practice it will be found that there are many 'short cuts' once the principal lines have been established.

Fig. 9.3 shows the plotting of circles in perspective. It is necessary to

HEIGHT LINE FOR RIDGE

HEIGHT LINE FOR WALLS

HEIGHT LINE FOR EAVES

EYE LEVEL

GROUND LINE

VP2.

VP1.

PICTURE PLANE

V.P.2.

PARALLEL TO
SIDE OF BUILDING

PLAN OF
GARAGE

ANGLE OF
VISION

90°

SPECTATOR

S

PARALLEL TO
SIDE OF BUILDING

V.P.1.

SETTING UP OF
MAIN LINES
(SOME CONSTRUCTION LINES
OMITTED FOR CLARITY)

PERSPECTIVE
OF A
SMALL GARAGE

Fig. 9.2

enclose them in a framework of straight lines, to set up the framework in perspective and then draw the curves through located points on the framework. Incidentally, circles on plan tend to become distorted in perspective, and better results can be obtained by drawing ellipses or part ellipses by eye once the general positions of the curves have been plotted.

In many other ways, too, it will be discovered that details can often be approximated in perspective by eye with far more satisfactory results than by a rigid adherence to the mechanical method of setting-up, as no method is completely free from distortion. And generally, apart from exercises in the subject, the aim of perspective drawing is to give as true a picture of the actual building as possible. But only practice and experience can provide the knowledge that enables these improvisations to be made, and the beginner should not take liberties too soon, to avoid the risk of getting into a hopeless tangle.

Fig. 9.4 illustrates a perspective view set up by the above method of the small house shown in orthographic projection in Figs. 7.28 and 7.29.

The foregoing method of perspective projection is known as 'two-point perspective' and is used for buildings generally. Another method of projection, which is more suitable for interior views or for the surroundings of a building seen in a straight elevation view, is known as 'one-point' or 'parallel' or 'interior' perspective, and the principle is illustrated in Fig. 9.5.

The basis is the same as for the method already described. Fig. 9.5, shows how the projection is made. In Fig. 9.5 (1), AD, BC, EH, FG is the plan of a room or part of a room; S is the position of the 'eye' of the spectator looking directly into the room. The picture plane is taken in the same plane as the end wall of the room, i.e. plane ABCD. On plan, lines are drawn from S through the near corners of the room, EH and FG, to contact the picture plane. The elevation of the end wall, ABCD, is now drawn to scale immediately above the plan, and the height of the eye-level is determined and a horizontal line accordingly drawn across it. Where the direct line of vision continued up from the plan cuts the eye-level is the vanishing point VP1 for 'all lines' running parallel to the direct line of vision. Therefore, by drawing lines from VP1 through A, B, C and D to contact the projection of EH and FG to the picture plane, the sides, floor and ceiling of the room in perspective are located.

Fig. 9.5 (2) shows how vertical and horizontal lines on the side walls are drawn. On plan, points L and M represent vertical 'lines' on the left-hand wall of the room, e.g. mullions or panelling. By drawing through these points from S and projecting perpendiculars upwards, the lines can be drawn in the correct positions on the side wall in perspective. KJ is a horizontal 'line' on the same wall; the height of it above the floor or the distance below the ceiling is known and is marked to scale along the corner of the room, AD, on the picture plane, and the line can then be drawn in perspective from VP1.

CIRCLES

HEIGHT LINE

e
d

c   EYE LEVEL

b
a

PERSPECTIVE

PICTURE
PLANE

PLAN

S

FRONT ELEVATION   SIDE

PERSPECTIVE
PROJECTION

Fig. 9.3

Fig. 9.4

Fig. 9.5 (3) shows the location of two points, O and P, on the floor and ceiling respectively. Their positions are marked on the plan and lines are drawn from them at 45° to the picture plane (for convenience one is taken to the left and one to the right). By reference to Fig. 9.5 (1) it will be seen how vanishing points, VP2 and VP3, are obtained for lines running at 45° across the plan. From the point where the line on plan from O cuts the picture plane a perpendicular is projected upwards to cut the bottom line of the end wall extended; through this intersection a line is drawn from VP2 to contact a line from VP 1 through the point where a perpendicular from O on plan cuts the end wall floor line, thus locating O in the perspective. Point P is found in a similar manner, the line of the ceiling level of the end wall being used in the construction.

Fig. 9.5 (4) shows a further stage illustrating in a similar manner the construction of, say, a book-case, QW, RU, SV, TX, projecting at right angles from the side wall.

The main lines or salient points of any pattern or object within the room can be plotted by the above methods in perspective.

In all perspective drawing the construction lines should be very light, but clearly and accurately drawn. The slightest error can easily become greatly exaggerated and upset the whole working. It is sometimes advisable to index points and lines on plan with letters or figures when they are numerous or close together in order to keep track of them. Always set up the main lines of the building or object first and work progressively from large to small details.

Perspective grids

Provided there is a clear understanding of the foregoing principles of perspective projections, which can only result from experiment and practice with various shapes and forms, much time and inconvenience can be saved in the initial setting out by tracing over predrawn grids. Fig. 9.6 shows such a grid for external two-point perspective projections made by the author some years ago.

The grid is set out in accordance with the method previously described for two sides of an assumed rectangular block as seen from an average viewing point, with one side 'vanishing' more rapidly than the other. Each side is divided into a reasonable number of equal squares. The lines of the divisions should not come too near together, and as they become closer or converge every alternate line is omitted. The lines may be continued to the left and right and upwards and downwards as may be necessary for whatever view is wanted, but it is probably best to confine the basic grid to the assumed block and to project any extensions on the individual settings out for particular subjects.

PERSPECTIVE

PLAN

DIRECT LINE OF VISION

I.

INTERIOR
PERSPECTIVE

Fig. 9.5

45°   45°

SPECTATOR   S

DIAGRAM

2.

3.

4.

VP

Grid can be reversed or used vertically
in either direction

lines can be extended as required

EYE LEVEL

Fig. 9.6

PERSPECTIVE GRID
ABOUT ONE-QUARTER ACTUAL SIZE

The grid can be drawn in pencil or ink in strong but not unduly thick lines on cartridge paper or heavy tracing paper or film, to a finished size of A1, although it may start out as a larger sheet in order to accommodate both vanishing points and the viewing point.

In use, the grid is pinned on the drawing board – if on tracing medium, over a clean white backing sheet – after adjustment as necessary to bring the eyelevel, which must be truly horizontal, to a position suitable for the required view: i.e. it may be higher or lower than normal, and similarly the grid may be moved nearer to one side or other of the board. If it is desired to view the main face of the building or object from the left, the grid can be reversed. When the grid has been correctly positioned, a sheet of tracing paper is placed over it, and after the ratio of the squares to the mensural scale of plan and elevation has been decided with regard to the overall size of the perspective projection, the setting-out for the final drawing can be ruled or drawn freehand using the grid as guidelines. Not all lines of the perspective will coincide with grid lines, but the positions of others and of plottings for curves, etc. can be fairly accurately estimated by reference to them.

The near angle of the building or object need not be taken as the corner of the assumed block; any existing vertical line may be used or an entirely new vertical line can be projected. In combination, therefore, with the variable position of the eye-level, a considerable range of views is possible. For tall buildings the board, and with it the grid, can be turned to provide settings out for ground level and aerial viewing points.

It will be appreciated, however, that despite the versatility of the grid, it can only be used satisfactorily for establishing the main lines of perspective drawings, and it is usually better to remove the grid from under the tracing before proceeding to fill in details or to transfer to drawing paper for completion. Once key lines and points are determined there is little difficulty in working out the rest of the projection. To go on too long over the grid can result in confusion and error.

Similar grids can be drawn for typical one-point interior perspectives and two-point internal angle perspectives; also for axonometric and isometric projections. The use of grids is particularly convenient for illustrations of buildings and details of modular design.

Aids to perspective drawing

Transfer lines

A number of Letratone transfer sheets, referred to on page 220, consist of equally spaced lines radiating as it were from distant vanishing points. Drawings can be adapted to utilize these sheets, for use on repetitive lines

Fig. 9.7   Example of ruled ink line drawing. Interior view of remodelled dock-side warehouse. True-scale cross-section in conjunction with one-point perspective. Note use of transfer figures to give scale and life. Bush Buildinhg, Bristol, UI. (Reproduced by permission of JT Building Services Ltd; drawn by Michael Duckering)

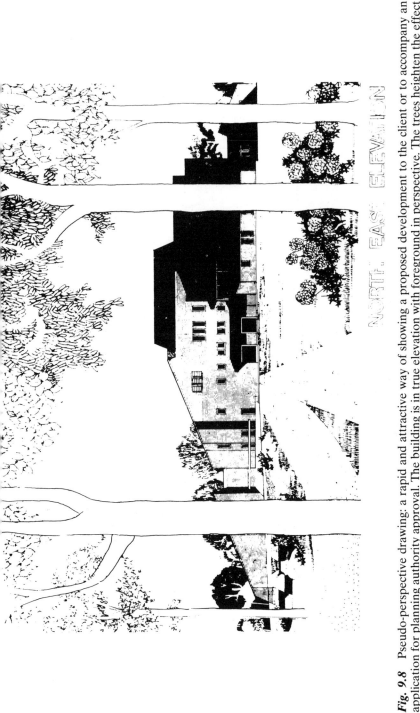

Fig. 9.8 Pseudo-perspective drawing: a rapid and attractive way of showing a proposed development to the client or to accompany an application for planning authority approval. The building is in true elevation with foreground in perspective. The trees heighten the effect of depth of foreground without obscuring the view of the building. Council offices, Tewkesbury, Building Partnership (Bristol) Ltd. Original in ink on tracing paper for dyeline printing; drawn by W. Spencer Tart.

Fig. 9.9   Example of freehand black lines made with 0.3 and 0.6 drawing pens on tracing sheet over accurately set-up cutaway interior perspective view of open-plan office building. Sectional tone applied by pressure transfer. The simplicity of the drawing technique was dictated in this instance by reproduction requirements. The technique is well suited to dyeline printing. (Graham Moss)

such as courses of brickwork or horizontal timber cladding. The main advantage lies in the absolute accuracy of the spacing.

Photography

Photographs can be used in several ways. They can be taken of the actual site and its surroundings to show existing features, background, details and colours, which can then be realistically but selectively used in the rendering of the perspective drawing. In some cases, a photograph can be taken from the desired viewpoint and the appropriate eye level and vanishing points can be approximated from a print. In other instances, the drawn and rendered subject perspective can be imposed upon a photographic enlarge-

Fig. 9.10 Proposed redevelopment at Bath Street on part of Coutage's Brewery site, Bristol (David Eccles).

ment of the site in such a way as to give a reasonably accurate impression of how the proposed development will actually appear when carried out. The effect can be given added realism by photographing the montage and producing a second-stage picture. The utilization of closely identified photographs and drawings is termed *photoperspective*. Procedures are comprehensively described in *Architectural Delineation* by Ernest Burden, published by McGraw-Hill.

10
Rendering and Presentation Techniques

Design drawings can be 'rendered': that is, coloured or otherwise treated in a number of different ways employing various media and techniques with the object of explaining the design more clearly than is possible by a line drawing only. One of the first aids in this respect is the showing of shades and shadows, which bring out the three-dimensional forms and the relationship of the various planes of the building or object to which they are applied.

Shadow projection

In architectural drawings the addition of shades and shadows on buildings is made according to the convention that the sun or source of light illuminates downwards from the left-hand side at an angle of 45° to the horizontal in elevation, and across at 45° to the front of the building in plan. Fig. 10.1 illustrates the principle by means of axonometric and orthographic drawings. The rays of light are assumed to be parallel.

The convention is a reasonable one as it corresponds to average natural conditions, and has the advantages of (1) giving shadows the width and height of which are in most cases the same as the projection or recess causing them, and (2) making the plotting easy, as it can be done entirely with T-square and a set square set to 45°. There is, however, no reason why the parallel motion or angle should not be varied, e.g. made 60°, if this would avoid confusion with other lines on the drawing, although this problem seldom arises.

Usually the projection of shades and shadows is made from elevation and plan, but sometimes it is necessary to work from elevation and section or side elevation.

The following examples illustrate the application of the principle to various geometrical solids, which are analogous to building forms. It is only by working out such examples that the method can be really grasped.

AXONOMETRIC

45°

35°/6'

45°

PARALLEL RAYS
OF LIGHT
AT 45° DOWNWARDS
FROM THE LEFT

HORIZONTAL
PLANE
(LEVEL GROUND)

SHADOW
PROJECTION

Fig. 10.1

ELEVATION

PARALLEL RAYS
OF LIGHT
AT 45° ACROSS
FROM THE LEFT

ORTHOGRAPHIC

PLAN

Fig. 10.2 (1) shows the shadow cast by an upright square prism (post) on horizontal (ground) and vertical (wall) planes as seen in the axonometric. Lines at 45° are drawn on elevation from the top corners of the prism in the direction of the light rays, and in a similar manner from the corners of the prism on plan. Where the lines on plan contact the vertical plane, perpendiculars are projected up to intersect the lines drawn on elevation and thus the outlines of the shadow are plotted. The various points are indexed on the drawing for clarity. If the prism had been far enough in front of the vertical plane its shadow would have fallen wholly on the horizontal plane. Its position would be found by projecting perpendiculars down from the points on the horizontal plane in elevation cut by the 45° lines from the top of the prism.

The sides of the prism away from the light source are in shade. The difference between shade and shadow is as follows. *Shade* occurs on a surface when because of its position in relation to the direction of the rays of light, it receives diminished light or no light at all. Shadow is that part of a surface receiving no direct light because some object comes between it and the source of light.

Fig. 10.2 (2) shows the casting of the shadow of an upright cylinder in a position similar to that of the prism. The shadow outline of the top has to be found by enclosing it in a square, by plotting the square in shadow and by then drawing through the common points of square and circle a smooth freehand curve, actually an ellipse. Part of the shade of the cylinder appears in the elevation. This is found by projecting up from the tangent point where a 45° line touches the circle representing the cylinder on plan. Although shown as a straight line dividing surfaces of light and dark on elevation, there would be no such hard division but a gradual change from the lightest part of the cylinder to the darkest. On small-scale drawings, however, it is usual to rule the line and darken to the right-hand side of it.

Fig. 10.2 (3) shows the shadow of an octagonal prism, and Fig. 10.2 (4) the shadow of a cone worked out on similar lines. In the case of the cone, note that the shadow position of the apex is first plotted on plan regardless of the vertical plane, and from the point so obtained lines, which define the shadow, are drawn to touch the base of the cone. From these points lines are drawn to the centre of the cone on plan to give the area of shade. Where the shadow lines meet the vertical plane project up to find the shadow on elevation.

Figs. 10.3 (1, 2 and 3) are examples of shadows cast by a square block on top of a square or rectangular prism, an octagonal prism and a cylinder. The construction lines are shown so that the plotting can be followed. Notice in regard to (1) that it is only necessary to draw down at 45° from the bottom left-hand corner of the block to the left-hand side of the prism in elevation, and then to draw a horizontal line across the prism. For proof, any point, A,

1. ELEVATION
VERTICAL PLANE
PLAN
SQUARE PRISM

2. CYLINDER

AXONOMETRIC

3. OCTAGONAL PRISM

4. CONE

Fig. 10.2

on the shadow-casting edge of the block can be plotted in shadow and it will be found to lie along the horizontal line. In (2) note the effect on the shadow caused by the corner of the block falling in shadow on the face of the prism is at right angles to the direction of the light rays. In (3), the shadow of the corner of the block is plotted on the surface of the cylinder, and a convenient number of points are likewise taken along the lower shadow-casting edge of the front of the block and are similarly plotted. A curve has then to be drawn through these points. The line of the shadow cast by the lower left-hand return edge of the block appears as a straight line at 45° in elevation. This can be proved by casting the shadows of any number of points on the edge on to the cylinder. The shadow cast by any straight edge projecting out at right angles to the vertical plane and parallel to the horizontal plane always appears as a 45° line on elevation no matter how curved or broken the surface on which it falls. The shadow merges on the right with the shade of the cylinder. As previously mentioned, the shade is not really defined by a hard edge but gradually fades into the lighter portion of the surface.

Fig. 10.3 (4, 5 and 6), similar to the foregoing, show the shadows cast by circular blocks on top of a square or rectangular prism, an octagonal prism and a cylinder. In each case it is necessary to plot the shadow from a number of points taken along the shadow-casting edge.

Fig. 10.4 illustrates examples of shadows cast by projections at right angles to a surface (vertical plane) in elevation. These are the equivalents of the shadows cast by similar vertical solids as would be seen on plan, although the direction of the shadows in relation to the objects would then be the same as the direction of the light rays. The construction lines are shown as before. Note that the end of the cylinder appears as a circle in shadow and can be most easily drawn by plotting the centre.

Fig. 10.5 shows examples of shadows formed in recesses. The shadows are cast by the left-hand edge in each case. The simplest way to find the shadow in the circular recess is to plot the centre of the front edge of the recess as shown. The curve of the shadow in plan in this example cannot be plotted except at a very large scale; it is sufficient to plot its beginning from the 45° tangent to the recess on elevation and to draw back a flat curve to the point where the shadow on elevation begins.

In Fig. 10.6 are illustrated two typical examples of shadows cast by buildings with pitched roofs. It will be seen that if the pitch of the roof is less than 45° there is no shadow cast by any part of it.

Fig. 10.7 shows the shadow cast by a chimney stack on a pitched roof..The plotting is similar in principle to the previous examples in Fig. 10.2, but it is necessary to draw the section in order to find the positions where the projectors from the top of the stack strike the inclined surface. The procedure is to find the shadow on elevation from the elevation and section, and then to project down to find the shadow on plan. Note that on elevation the in-

Fig. 10.3

ELEVATION

PLAN

SQUARE
PRISM *AXONOMETRIC*

OCTAGONAL
PRISM

CYLINDER

PROJECTIONS

Fig. 10.4

ELEVATION

PLAN

SQUARE

OCTAGONAL

45°
TANGENT

CIRCULAR

RECESSES

Fig. 10.5

EXAMPLES OF SHADOW
PROJECTION

PITCHED ROOF
LESS THAN 45°

PITCHED ROOF
MORE THAN 45°

ELEVATION

PLAN

BUILDINGS WITH PITCHED ROOFS

Fig. 10.6

ELEVATION

SECTION

SLOPE OF
ROOF

PLAN

AXONOMETRIC

CHIMNEY STACK AND PITCHED ROOF

Fig. 10.7

clination of the shadow lines of the vertical corners of the stack is the same as the pitch of the roof.

Fig. 10.8 shows the shade on a horizontal cylinder and the shadow cast by it on the horizontal plane.

Fig. 10.9 shows the shade on a sphere and the shadow cast by it on the horizontal plane. The line of shade is the line of an oblique cut through the centre of the sphere at right angles to the rays of light. The geometrical setting-out is not shown here, but the line is drawn on plan and elevation. As in the case of shade on any curved surface this line merely marks the position of the change from diminished light to no light. The shadow cast by the sphere is found by plotting from convenient points on the shade line. The outline of the shadow is that of an ellipse.

The foregoing examples, if drawn out and carefully studied, provide a knowledge of shades and shadows sufficient to meet the normal requirements in the rendering of drawings of most buildings. Further examples of a complex nature would tend to carry the subject into the realm of an academic pastime without giving much further material help.

Fig. 10.10 shows the shadows on the elevation and plan of the small house in Fig. 7.28. Shadows on plan, which are often omitted, are usually taken back in the direction shown. Shadows on elevations are always shown with the sun in the same relative position to the drawing, irrespective of the actual aspects of the elevations.

Fig. 10.11 shows a copy of the perspective of the same house with shadows added. Shadows in perspective must be worked out in orthographic projection first and then either set up along with the rest of the perspective or added to the perspective by 'eye'.

It is always better to work out shadows on tracing paper over the top of orthographic projections and then when correct to transfer them to the finished drawing. This procedure avoids spoiling the latter by the many construction lines, etc., that are necessary. Plottings should always be made with as fine a line as possible.

Outline shadows can be completed in many ways, from carefully graded washes of water-colour to applied transfer tones. Sprayed, spattered or pastel shadows are often used on small-scale drawings. Except where a bold effect is required, the transparency of shadows should not be lost. Shades and shadows are never really solid opaque areas, but are affected by the nature of the surfaces on which they occur and by reflected light as described below.

Reflected light

Fig. 10.12 gives illustrations of the principle of reflected light as used in rendering and the effect it has on shades and shadows. Every surface that

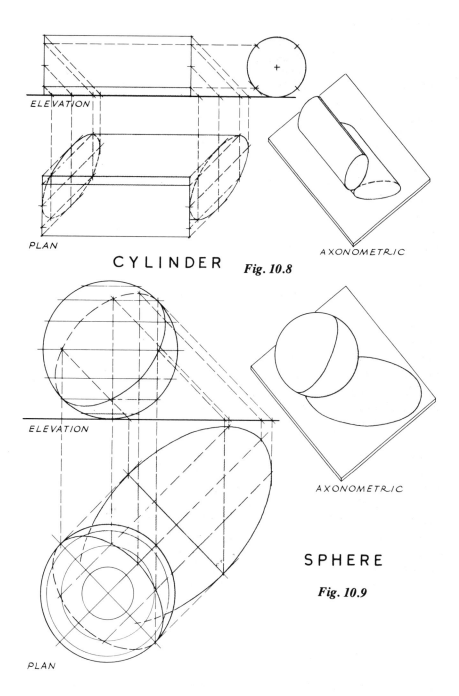

ELEVATION

PLAN

AXONOMETRIC

CYLINDER *Fig. 10.8*

ELEVATION

AXONOMETRIC

SPHERE

Fig. 10.9

PLAN

ELEVATION

PLAN

SHADOW PROJECTION

MAIN SHADOWS OF HOUSE SHOWN IN FIG. 7.29
FOR CLARITY SOME CONSTRUCTION LINES ARE OMITTED

Fig. 10.10

Fig. 10.11

receives direct light rays reflects the light to some extent and according to the angle or curvature in various directions. Consequently in bright sunlight reflected light falls on some of the surfaces that are in shade or shadow and alters their intensity and even casts shadows within shadows. The reflections are actually very complex, but just as there are conventional assumptions in regard to direct light so, for architectural drawings, reflected light rays are always assumed to be exactly the reverse of primary rays and to be appreciably weaker in value.

One effect of this, illustrated in Fig. 10.12 (1), is to vary the tones representing the shades and shadows: instead of their being rendered one tone all over, they are graded evenly in such a way that, in general, shadows are darker along their edges or outline and shades are darker where the surface receives no direct light and least reflected light.

Fig. 10.12 (2) illustrates how 'back shadows' – shadows within shadows – are cast by the rays of reflected light, and Fig. 10.12 (3) the effect of reflected light on the shadow within a deeply recessed opening.

As a general rule, no shade or shadow should be ungraded. Smooth grading helps considerably in giving 'life' to a rendering, and the sharper the grading and the greater the contrast between light and dark, the stronger the effect.

Long horizontal strips of shadow, e.g. under cornices, etc., which are too narrow to be graded with the lower edge darker can be successfully treated by making the left-hand end dark and grading off to the right.

Surroundings

The surroundings of a building, either actual or assumed, are often shown on rendered drawings to increase the realism of its presentation and to give 'scale', i.e. to give an impression of the real size of the building. To what extent this is necessary and in what manner it should be indicated, whether 'conventional' or 'naturalistic' for example, depends on the subject and the type of drawing desired. The simplest treatment consists in merely putting a graded background to the elevations, generally lighter towards the ground line, like a cloudless sky.

A basic conventional treatment for an isolated building is suggested by the sketches in Fig. 10.13. The treatment can be varied according to the technique used, scale of the drawing, etc. The first stage (1) is the putting of a dark band at the sides of the elevation to represent a hedge or fence, etc., behind it. This band, preferably graded darkest towards the building, sets it off and in conjunction with a graded sky above is quite effective. The second stage (2) shows a lighter and broader band above the first to represent a belt of trees some distance further back. Interest and probably contrast can be given to the regularity and squareness of most buildings by the addition

SHADOW APPEARS DARKER NEAR EDGES

SHADOW LIGHTENED BY REFLECTED LIGHT

ELEVATION

PLAN

RAYS OF REFLECTED LIGHT ASSUMED TO TRAVEL IN REVERSE DIRECTION TO PRIMARY RAYS

1

AXONOMETRIC

DIRECTION OF PRIMARY LIGHT RAYS

'BACK' SHADOWS

AXONOMETRIC

2

SHADOW APPEARS DARKER NEAR LOWER EDGE

RAYS OF REFLECTED LIGHT

ELEVATION

'BACK' SHADOW

ELEVATION

'BACK' SHADOW

PLAN LOOKING UP

DEEPLY RECESSED OPENINGS GRADED FROM DARK AT TOP TO LIGHT AT BOTTOM WHERE LIGHT REFLECTED FROM PAVING

3

'BACK' SHADOWS ARE CAST BY PROJECTIONS, ETC. WITHIN MAIN SHADOWS.

PRINCIPLES OF REFLECTED LIGHT AND 'BACK' SHADOWS

SHADOW PROJECTION

Fig. 10.12

of a tree to one side as shown in (3) and (4) and (6). A typical plan to correspond to such an arrangement is seen in (5).

The foreground is not included in the above examples, and many consider that to do so would be illogical in a purely elevational drawing, particularly if the facade of the building has any strong projections or recesses. It is fairly common, however, to show a foreground on such drawings in a semi-perspective manner as shown in Fig. 10.14. Sketches (1) and (2) illustrate the use of a vanishing point for converging lines of the foreground at normal eye-level on elevation. If the perspective effect is too acute with one central vanishing point, then two vanishing points equally spaced from the centre can be used, as in sketch (3)

The treatment of surroundings in perspective drawings can be freer and, in general, of a more naturalistic kind than in elevational drawings. Fig. 10.15 shows sketches typical of perspective compositions, although the possibilities and variations are limitless. Sketch (1) is an arrangement in perspective of the surroundings shown in Fig. 10.13 (3). The eye-level is more or less normal. Sketch (2), in which the eye-level is lower than normal, and therefore the amount of foreground should not be great, shows a composition for broader and more spacious effect with an interesting sky and view of distant landscape. Sketch (3) shows a building seen in aerial perspective. Careful attention must be paid here to the treatment of the ground, which receives greater prominence. Trees must be drawn correctly having regard to the viewpoint, and shadows are important elements in the composition.

Sky and clouds

A well-rendered sky greatly enhances the appearance of a good design, even if it will not wholly compensate for a poor design. The execution is, however, difficult at first and requires study and practice.

Fig. 10.16 illustrates some common types. After getting a grasp of these it is a matter of individual observation and experiment. A small pocket sketchbook is useful for noting down interesting skies from nature.

Sketch (1) shows the formal treatment usual with wash drawings. The sky is cloudless and graded from relatively dark at the top to light at the horizon. Although there are many different cloud effects in natural skies most 'architectural' skies can be dealt with either by the introduction of bunched cumulus clouds or of layers of stratus clouds. Sketch (2) shows the former and sketch (3) the latter, illustrating the general effect of each. Sketch (4) shows a perspective with clouds similar to (2), and sketch (5) a perspective with 'cirrus' clouds of a like character to (3), but having a more lively effect. Note how the clouds follow the lines of perspective.

By whatever technique the clouds are represented there are two important points to be borne in mind: (1) the edges of clouds are invarably

1. DARK BAND AT SIDE OF BUILDING TO REPRESENT HEDGE OR FENCE

2. ADDITION OF BROAD, LIGHT BAND TO REPRESENT BELT OF TREES BEHIND BUILDING

3. ADDITION OF TREE TO ONE SIDE ADDS INTEREST & GIVES CONTRAST TO BUILDING

4. APPLICATION OF 3. TO ASYMMETRICAL ELEVATION - POSITION AS REQUIRED FOR BALANCE.

5. TYPICAL PLAN REPRESENTATION OF 3. ABOVE

6. ALTERNATIVE ARRANGEMENT TO 4., ABOVE USING MASS OF DARK FOLIAGE

SURROUNDINGS *ELEVATIONS*

Fig. 10.13

1.

VANISHING
POINT AT
NORMAL EYE-
LEVEL ON
ELEVATION

2.

3.

FOREGROUND

Fig. 10.14

1.
CLOUDLESS
SKY

BELT OF TREES

HEDGE OR FENCE

TYPICAL COMPO-
SITION - OPEN SITE.
BUT EFFECT OF
ENCLOSURE

2.
SKY

CLOUDS

DARK FOLIAGE
TO SET OFF
BUILDING AND
GIVE CONTRAST

DISTANT LANDSCAPE

FOREGROUND MUST NOT
BE MORE THAN SHOWN

COMPOSITION
FOR BROADER,
SPACIOUS EFFECT

3.
CLUMP OF TREES
(TREES & DETAIL
MUST AGREE WITH
VIEW POINT).

SHADOWS ARE
IMPORTANT

AERIAL VIEW.

SURROUNDINGS *PERSPECTIVES*

Fig. 10.15

1. NORMAL CLOUDLESS SKY USUALLY EVENLY GRADED FROM DARK AT TOP TO LIGHT HORIZON - FORMAL TREATMENT.

DARKER SKY

LIGHT BUT GRADED SKY

2. ELEVATION WITH BUNCHED MASSES OF CUMULUS CLOUDS 'LIVELY' EFFECT.

3. ELEVATION WITH LAYERS OF STRATUS CLOUDS. 'REPOSEFUL' EFFECT.

4. PERSPECTIVE WITH CLOUDS AS IN 2.

5. PERSPECTIVE WITH CIRRUS-TYPE CLOUDS.

SURROUNDINGS SKY & CLOUDS   *Fig. 10.16*

soft, and (2) clouds are just as much elements in the general composition as anything elseóthe sky must not be such a *tour de force* as to overpower the building.

Trees

Most architectural renderings include trees of one kind or another. As with clouds, there are many different types and many ways of drawing them, both conventional and naturalistic. Again, too, it is largely a matter of observation and experiment on the part of each individual.

Fig. 10.17 shows the drawing of various types of tree. These have been drawn in soft pencil, and the drawing would be modified for other media. In the top left-hand corner is the tree that often occurs on the beginner's early drawings, but fortunately nowhere else. Two conventional types of trees are shown next in elevation and plan based on circles and squares; their use is restricted to formal renderings where it is desirable not to disturb the strictly architectural lines of the drawing. In the right-hand top corner is a more natural representation, which might be sescribed as a 'general purpose' tree.

As one of the reasons for putting trees on drawings is to help express the actual size of the building, the trees themselves must be to scale. When the representation is obviously that of a full-grown oak somewhere near to the building, for example, it is absurd to find it scaling 3 or 4 metres in height. The sketches on the second row of the figure shows sizes of certain types of trees compared to that of a man.

Points to be borne in mind in drawing trees are:

- Trees must look as if they are growing out of the ground, not floating, in the air. An indication of the swelling towards the roots, and shadows, are helpful in this respect.
- If a tree is meant to represent a particular species, it must lock something like that species.
- Trees should never appear to be growing out of roofs. Isolated trees behind a building are best omitted, unless they can be related to similar trees, the whole of which can be seen at the sides of the building.
- The trunk and branches must seem able to support the foliage.
- The foliage must appear to be rounded, not as if cut out of cardboard.
- Trees should not be overdrawn and laboured, especially if they are to be coloured. A suggestion of the main lines is sufficient.
- Near trees in perspective are seen in more detail than distant ones, which can be resolved into mass only.

ELEVATIONS

CONVENTIONAL TREES
FOR FORMAL EFFECT

PLANS

TREES MUST BE IN SCALE WITH SCALE OF DRAWING.

DENSE
FOLIAGE

SPRING
FOLIAGE

DISTANT
TREES

SILVER BIRCH

BUSHES

YOUNG
TREE

SHRUBS

GROUND SHADOWS IMPORTANT
IN PERSPECTIVE

SURROUNDINGS *TREES*

Fig. 10.17

Human figures, vehicles etc.

In addition to trees, which may not be appropriate to the subject, other elements used in both orthographic and perspective drawings to give scale and realism include human figures, cars, street furniture, lamp standards, etc. Adjoining or adjacent buildings or other structures can also be shown, and indeed should be shown if the design relationship is important; if a particular site is concerned, sketches should be made on the spot or photographs taken to provide a basis for more or less accurate indication.

As a general principle, whatever additional elements are introduced, they must be subordinate to the main subject. They must be kept simple and in some cases reduced to conventional or even abstract forms. All the elements must be arranged to produce a satisfactory composition and, reinforcing the design, lead the eye to a focal point – often the entrance to the building.

Human figures in particular need special care both in placing and in delineation. Only if it is necessary to convey the building's function should large numbers of figures or vehicles be shown. Usually, a few groups of two or three figures and an individual here and there are sufficient. In perspective drawings the figures are best placed near the building, some at the entrance, in correct relative sizes according to their positions. Over-size figures must be avoided, and the temptation to add foreground or 'head and shoulders' figures should be resisted.

There are many ways of drawing figures but uniformity of representation on any one drawing is essential. The student should study the work of others while developing his own style. Figures need not be amorphous blobs, but detailed realism is seldom justified and may detract from the overall effect. Extreme fashions in clothing, etc. are unsuitable as they draw too much attention, and also date quickly; caricature of any kind is out of place. Similarly, cars and aircraft should be drawn with a degree of anonymity. However, boats and sailing craft are less likely to change and can be more precisely drawn in connection with waterside buildings.

As well as the foregoing pictorial effects, use may be made of foreground shadows from assumed buildings or trees outside the picture, of reflections on wet roads or pavings, and of internal and external illumination.

Standard pictorial symbols

Although personally drawn trees, human figures, cars etc. have greater character, can be more satisfactorily integrated, and make possible infinite variations of treatment and style, standard graphic symbols can be used for convenience, uniformity, and sometimes speed. They may be of the pressure-transfer type. Symbols to correspond to various scales are obtainable and can be applied equally well to final drawings in orthographic projection or to tracing media for photoprint reproduction. The tree plan symbols are particularly useful for layouts, landscape and town-planning drawings.

For elevations and sections, standard symbols must be apposite and selected with care. Indiscriminate and unrestrained use of inappropriate symbols, no matter how attractive they are in themselves, will impart at best only a superficial and temporary appeal to the drawing, and at worst will degrade the design and confuse the presentation. However, if the symbols are regarded as basic elements of pictorial composition for imaginative manipulation, they can be of considerable help to the draughtsman in preparing formal drawings.

Paper for drawings in wash

Drawings that are made in line only or which are rendered in one of the 'dry' media – pastel, crayon, etc. – can be made on paper that is pinned to the drawing board, but if washes of Chinese ink or water-colour are to be used, or if the drawing is to be sprayed, then it is necessary to use mounted or stretched paper, which will not cockle when wet. Mounted papers or boards such as Saunders, and fashion-plate, are reasonably satisfactory for most work in water-colour and gouache. But they have disadvantages for both initial pencil drawing, if extensive, and prolonged rendering in wash, being less 'sympathetic' than stretched paper and less capable of standing up to sponging. Therefore, although the operation is admittedly messy and time-consuming, the method of stretching paper is described below. The paper must be handmade, the thicker the better; HP (hot pressed) or smooth is generally suitable.

1. The right side of the paper is found by holding it up to the light so that the watermark can be read.
2. The paper is laid on the board with the right side uppermost and the edges are turned up about 20 mm to form a shallow tray.
3. The paper is then turned over and with a sponge water is applied around the edges up to the folding mark-the 20 mm strip not being wetted as this is later to be pasted. The sponge is next applied diagonally and to the main axes, union jack, fashion, and these bands are thoroughly wetted. The whole sheet, except the pasting strip, is then wetted and allowed two or three minutes for the water to to soak in. Any standing water is removed at the end of that time.
4. The paper is turned back right side uppermost, the edges are made square with the board, and water is liberally applied to the upper surface parti-

cularly around the edges which were not wetted on the underside. After this operation the paper should be covered with buckles and pools of water.

5. Paste is now quickly applied to the outside dry edges of the underside, starting with one of the short sides. When all the edges are pasted, some of the standing water can be removed but a pool must be left in the middle. The edges of the paper are again adjusted square with the board. The middle of the short side first pasted is then taken, pressed firmly down and with thumb and fingers pulling and pressing the edge is stuck to the board along to the corners. The opposite edge of the paper is then lifted carefully and slightly by the corners and pulled gently so as to free the underside of the paper from moisture-adhesion to the board. It is then stuck down as before, pulled strongly by the fingers first at the middle and then outwards to the corners. The two short edges now being held, the long edges are stuck down in the same way, starting at the middle and working to the corners, pulling and pressing until the whole sheet is flat and firmly stuck down all round.

An extra pressing can be given to the stuck edges by means of a hard but smooth object such as the handle of a knife or a coin edge, etc. If the paste is satisfactory nothing more is necessary in this respect, but if any doubt is felt, drawing pins can be put in at weak points or at intervals around the sheet after the edge has been dried off a little with a clean cloth. Or, alternatively, strips of adhesive paper can be stuck around the sheet, half on the paper and half on the board.

When the sheet is satisfactorily stuck down, all standing water on the surface is removed with the sponge, and the paper is mopped off gently without scrubbing from the edges inwards so that the part to dry last is the middle.

The process of drying cannot be hastened without risk, and until all signs of dampness have disappeared the board must be kept horizontal. Time for drying will depend upon a number of factors. It can be lessened by placing the board in a draught, either near an open window but away from direct sunlight and soot specks or from an electric fan. If the drying is done too quickly the paper may split or come off.

If, for any reason, the edges of the paper or the tape have to be turned down over the edges of the board, they must be trimmed off afterwards with a sharp knife or razor blade to allow the T-square to run smoothly.

Sometimes, even with every care, the sheet comes off altogether or in part while drying, or fails to dry out properly, leaving ridges and buckles. If the drawing is to be an important one, the only thing to do in such cases is to start afresh with a new sheet of paper, although if the first sheet is not damaged it can be used again for another drawing.

If it is a case of slight ridging – usually in the corners – and a large number of big washes are not required, then by thoroughly wetting the surface of the paper and allowing it to dry out again very likely the ridges will disappear. The paper will at best, however, be only lightly stretched and the running of washes will cause it to buckle temporarily and may prove a nuisance.

If the sheet comes off along one or two sides only, and is otherwise firmly held, the stretching can often be made good. The underside should first be wetted as far as possible with the exception of the pasting strip; then the top surface is thoroughly wetted and the water allowed to soak in. New paste is applied and the sheet firmly stretched and stuck down once more and allowed to dry out slowly.

Rendering in wash

As an introduction to all kinds of rendering, that using washes is of the greatest value. While its practice is less extensive than at one time it is still suitable for formal drawings of a dignified character, either alone or in combination with other techniques. Exercises in wash rendering are the surest guide to all the basic principles, and provide excellent discipline for the hand and eye.

The first step, after the completed line drawing in pencil has been carefully checked, is to clean it up if necessary, and then to give it a wash of water over the whole sheet. The purpose of this is not, as is sometimes thought, to remove the ingrained dirt from the paper, but to remove any loose pencil dust, grease from the hands, etc., and, most of all, to overcome dryness in the paper, especially if it has been exposed on the board for a long time. This water wash also has the effect of 'fixing' the pencil lines to some extent, making them more difficult to rub out, which is why the checking must be done before.

Next, the shades and shadows (see page. 178) are worked out on tracing paper and transferred to the drawing. A further water wash may then be given, but is optional. Some draughters mix a very little alum with the water washes (one tablespoonful to a quart of water) as this is supposed to help remove grease and make the later washes run better.

Water washes are put on like any other wash, and the procedure is illustrated in Fig. 10.18. The board should be tilted slightly, not more than about 1 in 10 or about 5°. The upper end is best supported on a suitable block of wood rather than on unsteady books, etc. The way up of the board depends on the area to be dealt with. Generally, it is easier to work with the lesser dimension running horizontally: for example in the case of an overall wash, the board would be as shown in Fig. 10.18.

Elementary laying of washes

Washes must always be run from the highest part to the lowest. The procedure is to fill the brush –wash brush, page 17, for large areas – and start along the upper edge of the area, putting on a good deal of the liquid, working it carefully to the top line.[1] Then, by means of long regular horizontal brush strokes with short vertical ones at the sides, bring the wash down the sheet or area, keeping it evenly wet all the time. The brush should not 'paint' the paper but merely touch the raised edge of the wash and guide it along.

It is particularly important with washes of heavy water-colour to work slowly and smoothly, or the deposit of the colour will be irregular and unpleasant.

When the wash has been brought to the bottom of the area it must be finished off carefully along the line, and this is sometimes more easily effected with a smaller size of brush, say No. 6. The wash will tend to collect at the bottom, and the surplus must be gently removed by holding a squeezed-out brush just touching it so that the liquid is drawn up into the hairs. This operation is repeated as many times as necessary to ensure that the wash dries evenly from the top downwards.

If properly put on, a wash should show a perfectly regular tone, colour or mottle over the whole area.

If the wash is in two parts for a distance, e.g. passing on either side of an elevation, as in Fig. 10.19, the two parts must be kept moving equally and evenly. It is easier in such cases to start with the divided parts, doing a bit to each in turn.

Brushes loaded with water or wash should not be carried over the drawing any more than necessary because of possible drops. (Fig. 10.18).

Above all, washes must be run 'wet'. There must be enough wash mixed up at the beginning to cover the whole area; it is fatal to have to stop in the middle of putting on a wash to mix up some more.

Defects in wash rendering

The following are the defects most likely to occur in wash rendering. They should be guarded against so far as possible, but can sometimes be remedied as described.

---

[1] It is, of course, unnecessary to work to border lines if the sheet is to be cut off along them afterwards.

TONE VALUE

Fig. 10.20

Untidy Edges

Caused when the wash over-runs or falls short of the enclosing lines. To remedy, when the wash is dry, take a small brush, dip it in clean water and dampen the edges affected and blot them off with clean blotting paper several times until all traces of the over-run or the sharp edges of the short wash are removed. This matter should be attended to after every wash, should the defects not allowed to accumulate. Stubborn over-runs can be quickly cleaned off by holding a piece of thin card (postcard) along the true edge of the wash and taking a small piece of sponge dipped in clean water, wiping away gently the over-run.

Blots

Caused by drops of colour falling on the rendered parts of the drawing. If blotted up immediately – a piece of clean blotting paper should always be handy, but sacrifice a handkerchief if necessary – nothing may show. If the marks have been overlooked and have dried, take a bluntish brush and clean water and gently wash over the spots repeatedly with alternate blottings until they are light enough to be blended in as described later.

Run-backs

Result from a collection of wash at the bottom of an area seeping back up the partially dried upper part or, sometimes, from the addition of a quantity of wash to an area that has been run rather on the dry side. If serious, nothing much can be done to remedy this defect and the whole area may have to be sponged out with clean water when quite dry. In less serious cases, the specks of pigment that float back can be picked out carefully with the point of a brush and the worst effects are somewhat mitigated. In free water-colour renderings, run-backs are sometimes deliberately sought to build up a striking effect, but this is no trick for beginners.

Streaks

Horizontal lines of darker colour are usually caused by running the wash too slowly or unevenly, or by a defect in the paper – spoiled surface due to previous-rubbing out – or impurities in the wash. If serious, lift the board and with sponge and clean water gently sponge over the area, trying to remove the streaks. Do not start sponging until the area is dry all over. Avoid scrubbing the surface or it will be ruined. Streaks are less likely to occur with light washes, and for formal drawings tones should be built up by a succession of washes. Sometimes the streaks can be turned to account, if occurring in the 'sky', by being made into clouds.

Grease Spots

Small spots that refuse to take colour are due to some sort of grease or water-repellent having affected the fibres of the paper. If not too large, these can be patched up to match the rest of the wash by stippling on colour with the point of a small brush or by cross-hatching, or with the point of a small brush much in the manner of darning. With patience and a steady hand almost 'invisible repairs' can be made. The airbrush can also be used for this work.

Sponging off

Reference has been made to the sponging off of defective washes; it is also a useful procedure to soften the tones of a rendering in Chinese ink or water-colour and to remove any hard edges. The sponging should always be done when the drawing is evenly dry all over, with a maximum of clean water and the minimum of scrubbing.

General procedure with wash drawing

Rendering should follow an orderly sequence and should proceed evenly over the whole sheet. It is bad practice to render up one portion of a drawing, completely before the rest; the result is bound to be patchy.

A scheme of tones should be determined at the beginning. This can be worked out by means of thumbnail sketches in soft pencil. The big washes should be put on first, starting with the general tones, then the lesser ones gradually working down to the final accents. A light even tone to establish shade and shadow areas can be applied at an early stage with advantage; later the tones can be strengthened and graded as necessary.

Generally, unless the area is very small, it is better to build up tone value by a series of washes rather than to try and do it in one wash. By building up gradually the correct tonal relationships between the various parts can be maintained more closely and the desired balance systematically achieved, whereas to get correct final tones by single washes, although possible and quicker, requires considerable experience.

Tones should be carefully related in strength to create the illusion of perspective in an elevational drawing, to get the effect of light and shade on the building, and to emphasize the composition of the picture. There should be a scheme of tones whereby distant planes appear to recede in a logical sequence. Usually the foremost facade of the building is the lightest tone, the vertical planes behind it getting darker the further away they are (Fig. 10.20 (3)), but the flanking parts of an elevation may be kept dark to avoid taking the interest away from the centre. For example, if the building is

U-shaped with projecting wings the order of the tones might be reversed.

The strengths of shades and shadows and accents generally should be most intense on the lightest plane, concentrating in effort at the visual centre of interest, and getting relatively weaker on successive darker planes.

If the foreground is a more or less horizontal plane it should be graded from dark at the bottom of the picture to light near the principal face of the building. It should also be somewhat darker at the sides. The building will appear to 'float' if the foreground is too dark (Fig. 10.20).

The sky should be graded, even if later broken up by clouds, for relatively dark at the top to light at the horizon (Fig. 10.20 (1)) except in the case of very tall buildings, when a better effect is sometimes obtained by grading in the reverse way (Fig. 10.20 (2)).

Graded washes should be applied to inclined planes, such as roofs, to give contrast with adjoining areas. Usually, steep pitched roofs should be darker towards the top; flat pitched roofs darker towards the eaves.

It is advisable to grade all principal washes. The picture is thereby greatly enlivened and corresponds more closely to reality. The building should be graded to heighten the contrast with its surroundings and to acknowledge the effects of reflected light, i.e. lighter towards the bottom if paving or light ground, darker towards the bottom if dark grass, etc. The grading should be gentle. Shades and shadows should also be graded.

Media

The principal media used for rendering drawings are:

- Chinese ink washes.
- Water-colours.
- Gouache and Poster colours.
- Pastel.
- Coloured pencils.
- Water-colour pencils
- Pencil only or black ink only.
- Aerosol spray colours
- Dry transfer tones and colours.

All of these can be used by themselves or in combination with one or more of the others. It must be emphasized again that it is by personal handling of these materials and the study of actual drawings that the full possibilities of each will be realized. It is not attempted here to do more than give a few suggestions and hints.

LAYING A WASH

BLOTTING PAPER

TILT OF BOARD FOR ORDINARY
PURPOSES

ABOUT 5 DEGS. OR 1:10

Fig. 10.18

DIVIDED WASH
BROUGHT DOWN
EVENLY ON EITHER
SIDE OF "BUILDING"

Fig. 10.19

Fig. 10.21

ALTERNATIVE
METHODS OF
FILTERING
CHINESE
STICK INK

A

B

Fig. 10.22

CHINESE STICK

Chinese ink

Chinese ink can still be obtained in colour sticks usually marked with Chinese characters. There are various sizes, but quite a small one will last some time. The quality also varies, the cheaper being rather harsh and cold in tint; the more expensive is warmer and is always to be preferred. The particular value of the ink is its transparency, which gives to a formal wash drawing a finish difficult to obtain by other means. It is especially useful for early exercises in wash rendering and for neutral washes on any kind of drawing.

The ink is prepared for use by being rubbed down with a little water on a slate slab or in a saucer (Fig. 10.21). If a quantity of wash is required it is advisable to rub down a strong mixture – almost black in intensity when tried out on a piece of paper – which can be subsequently diluted as needed. The liquid must be filtered after being rubbed down, by being passed through fine muslin or coarse filter paper until all specks are removed. An alternative filtering process is to soak a small piece of string in water and, by putting one end in a saucer at a lower level and the other end in a saucer of the ink at a higher level, to allow it to pass through by capillary attraction. This action filters it at the same time (Fig. 10.22).

The filtering process is of the greatest importance and must be carried out carefully. The filtered ink can be stored in a clean bottle with a clean stopper or covered over with damp blotting paper for several days.

After use the colour stick should be wiped dry or it will crack and become useless.

The ink should be used in light washes, dark tones being gradually built up, the general procedure being as described for wash rendering. The ink dries much lighter than it appears when wet. Water-colours, such as cobalt blue, viridian, burnt sienna, raw sienna, and carmine, can be added in small quantities to tint the ink if desired

Water-colours

Some reference has already been made to water-colours, (page 16). For formal rendering in wash it is usual to work with mixtures of burnt sienna and french ultramarine, or raw sienna and ivory black, or cobalt blue and light red. These mixtures should be definitely inclined in hue towards one or other of the constituents. In all cases, the colours are deposited as the wash is run, forming what is termed a 'mottle', and it is by the speed and manipulation of the brush that the most interesting effects are obtained. Knowledge of this can only come by experiment. It is essential, of course, that the wash is put on evenly and kept very wet. And, as the pigments tend to be deposited in the jar or dish, the wash must be stirred up every time a

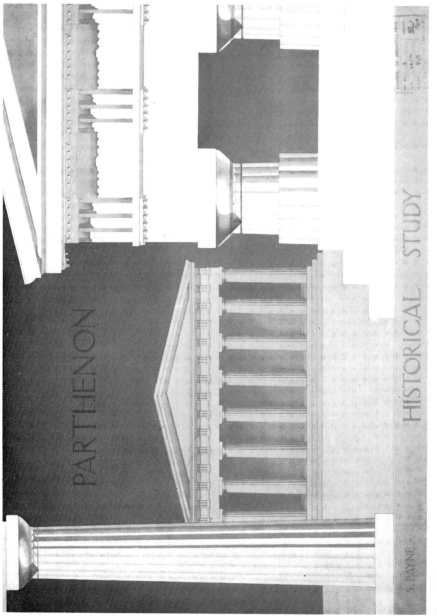

Fig. 10.23   Drawing in pencil and Chinese ink washes (Sylvia Payne).

brushful is taken. As with Chinese ink, if a good quantity of colour is required, it is better to mix the whole lot at the beginning rather than have the difficult task of mixing new washes to match the original at various times.

It is not possible to discuss free water-colour rendering in detail. Watercolour is perhaps the most flexible medium of all, and can be used with success for every type of drawing. Experiments should be made at first with a few colours, and then new ones can be added to the palette and others discarded according to individual preference. A wide range is seldom necessary; many successful water-colourists manage with about half a dozen only.

A few hints are: avoid Prussian blue and vandyke brown, which stain the fibres of the paper and cannot be sponged out if anything goes wrong. Never mix ultramarine and vermilion; a chemical reaction produces a black sediment. Always put the colours on wet, except for an occasional dry brush stroke for foreground treatment or other special effect. Try to let the colours do the work. Avoid 'painting' them on thickly and muddily; let the white of the paper show here and there for highlights and sparkle. Vivid colours should be reserved for accents and spots of interest; large patches of them are garish. Cobalt is the best blue for skies. Burnt sienna with a little ultramarine is better for brickwork than any red. Raw sienna is a useful colour for light tones on stonework, etc.

Gouache and poster colours

Opaque colours (see page 16) are the equivalent of water-colours mixed with Chinese white. They dry with a flat matt surface of even tone if properly applied, and because of this are often used to represent buildings of simple form and sharp outlines, and particularly for interior design drawings. It is essentially a medium for strong if not bold effects.

The colours can be used in combination with water-colour or with pastel: for example, a building largely coloured in poster colour with a water-colour or pastel sky. The colour must not be too wet when applied to the paper or it will not dry evenly. A second coat must be applied fairly dry or excess water will be absorbed by the first, which will mix with the second or be pulled off by the brush. For large areas of thick colour, which are to be gone over owing to alterations, it is safer to remove the first coat with a knife or with a wet brush and blotting paper. If the colour is applied too thickly it may flake off when dry. Small but regular areas of colour can be outlined with the ruling pen and filled in with the brush before the lines are dry. Brick courses can also be ruled in to small scales. Poster colour or Chinese white can be superimposed over indian ink, but indian ink cannot be superimposed on either of the former. Fine detail can often be effectively added to poster colour by drawing on it with a sharp HB pencil, the line appearing with unusual brilliance. Although poster colour covers up original pencil lines, this should not be made an excuse for careless draughting.

If designers' colours are used, the following are useful colours that will meet most requirements: black, white, indigo, lemon yellow, red ochre, raw sienna, vandyke brown, geranium red.

Pastel

Pastel is used in architectural rendering for applying soft, graded tones and colours to the comparatively larger areas of the drawing. The method in general (Fig. 10.24) is to scrape off with a penknife or to crush a small quantity of pastel on to a sheet of cartridge paper, known as the rubbing sheet, until a very fine powder is obtained, and then to pick it up with a piece of cotton-wool and apply it to the drawing by firm even rubbing, the parts of the drawing not to be pastelled being masked by thin card or stiff paper.

Only the best pastels of finest grain should be used. There are many different colours and tones, so many that it is best to start with a representative selection and add and discard as suggested for water-colours. Strong, vivid colours are little used. Useful ones are: raw sienna, autumn brown, green grey, indian red, prussian green, white and black. The colours can be blended together on the rubbing sheet.

The medium lends itself well to sky effects, a wide range of soft tones being easily obtained. 'Breaks' can be made in the clouds by removing some of the pastel with a plastic rubber. The main tones on buildings can also be applied lightly with grading, and a suggestion of foreground can be given by rubbing off a little pastel downwards from the ground line of the elevation.

Pastel by itself is seldom sufficient and the accents of the rendering can be given by touches of poster colour, e.g. ruled window-bars, flowers, trees, figures, etc.

Trees can, however, be pastelled by cutting an irregular shape in a thin card and by rubbing through this to build up a mass of foliage, as shown in Fig. 10.25, the trunk and branches of the tree being added by thin brush strokes of dry poster colour dragged upwards from the ground.

The chief disadvantage of pastel is the amount of dust that gets on to hands, clothes, and sometimes, the wrong parts of the drawing.

Coloured pencils etc.

The use of coloured pencils is restricted in the main to good-sized drawings to a fairly large scale, although in combination with ordinary pencil or

BOX OF PASTELS

RUBBING SHEET

PLASTIC RUBBER

WAD OF COTTON WOOL

DIRECTION OF STROKES

Fig. 10.24

MASK TO SHIELD DRAWING

MASSES OF FOLIAGE FROM SAME STENCIL

CUTTING KNIFE FOR STENCILS, MASKS ETC.

RAZOR BLADE FOR CUTTING STENCILS, ETC.

IRREGULAR SHAPE CUT IN CARD FOR FOLIAGE OF TREE

PASTEL

Fig. 10.25

indian ink detail can be satisfactorily tackled. The advantage of using coloured pencils lies in the ease and speed of the medium and the wide range of tone values according to pressure. The technique can vary from free coloured sketching to quite formal renderings wherein regular, even tones are obtained by carefully ruled, close, parallel lines. The applying of colour and tone by indiscriminate scribbling must be avoided.

Crayons and chalks and felt-tipped pens can be similarly employed. For rapid, broad effects the best medium is charcoal. The sticks should be held almost parallel to the paper in use and not like a pencil. Tones can be obtained by smudging with the fingers.

Drawings in charcoal, crayon, or any powdery medium need to be protected on completion by being sprayed with a fixing liquid.

Water-colour pencils

The ability to present in water-colour without applying a wash with a brush in the traditional manner is a useful skill that can be easily acquired with water-colour pencils.

Soft water-soluble pencils combine pure consistent colour with maximum versatility. They are used dry as normal colour pencils and then washed over with a wet brush to achieve a true water-colour effect. They can also be used wet to produce a water-colour drawing.

This technique may also be applied to maps and diagrams where it is necessary to identify development locations and building sites, as well as on town planners' land maps.

Pencil

Pencil renderings in general consist of the addition of shadows and surroundings in line; shadows, for example, often being indicated by close parallel lines, either horizontal or vertical, according to the area concerned. Gradations of tone can be obtained by varying the pressure on the pencil and sometimes by cross-hatching. A little smudging by the finger, however, can be done to add indefinite tones for clouds, foliage, etc.

Lines of indian ink to the silhouette of the building or for accents and points of emphasis can be used on otherwise pencil drawings.

Pen and ink

Formal drawings completed wholly in pen and ink are very infrequent, the technique being more often used for freehand sketches on the lines described in Chapter 11. Small-scale elevations, however, can be effectively shown in ink with blacked-in openings and the addition of very simple surroundings in line.

Perspectives also must be fairly small to be successfully executed in ink. Large drawings in the medium, unless the brush supplements the pen, tend to look laboured and restless. The mapping pen, incidentally, generally gives too fine a line for any but the smallest drawings.

As variations of tone cannot be obtained directly with ink, greater use has to be made of different thickness of line, cross-hatching, dots, dashes and areas of solid black, and the possibilities of these should be thoroughly studied.

Sepia ink is a possible alternative to indian ink, and wash – sepia or ivory black water-colour – combined with ink drawing opens up wider fields of expression.

Spatter, spray, and airbrush techniques _____

Water-colour and Chinese ink, instead of being washed on with a brush, can be applied to drawings in the form of minute particles by the following methods.

Spatter

For small areas, especially shadows on 1:100 and 1:200 scale elevations, colour can be spattered on using a toothbrush or similar stiff brush and a piece of fine wire mesh, as shown in Fig. 10.26. The ink – indian ink is commonly used for shadows – or poster colour is mixed in a dish and picked up by the brush, which is then rubbed backwards and forwards over the mesh, held horizontally a short distance away from the paper. The brush must not be too wet or splashes will mar the fine texture that can otherwise be obtained. It is comparatively easy to grade evenly quite small areas by this method. Great care must be taken to mask all parts of the drawing not to be spattered, even those some distance away from the operation. The usual practice is to fit pieces of stiff paper carefully to the outlines concerned and to hold the edges flat with coins or similar small heavy articles. The slightest separation of the surfaces of the drawing and the mask will allow the spatter to find its way in and spoil the sharpness of the edge to which it should be confined.

Spray

For large areas, particularly skies, water-colour can be sprayed on, using a metal spray of the type sold for spraying fixing liquid on to charcoal drawings and costing only a few pence, as illustrated in Fig. 10.27, or an atomizer such as a throat spray. The particles of colour are much larger by this method; this may be an advantage for bold drawings.

It is again necessary to cover the parts of the drawing not to be sprayed, but as it is better to stand the board vertically, a mask or template is cut out of thick tracing paper or detail paper and held in position by ordinary pins about an inch apart close to the edge. The pins must be carefully placed so that the prick marks, which should be very slight, do not show afterwards. For small areas, which cannot be easily masked in this way, a coating of diluted rubber cement can be painted on and later removed quite cleanly.

The spray should be blown horizontally to the drawing from two or three feet away at least, so that any large, heavy drops fall clear of the drawing and only the finer particles impinge on the surface.

The spray should be kept steady in force and should be moved about to prevent any one part of the surface becoming too wet and causing the particles to run together. The process should not be rushed, but the mask must not be allowed to cockle or shrink. If the spray does, however, fall outside its intended limits, it can usually be washed off afterwards with a brush and clean water. It is said that a little alcohol added to the liquid gives a finer spray and quickens the drying.

The strength of the spray is difficult to judge until the mask is removed, but a corner can always be turned down at intervals and affords some guide.

Any colour can, of course, be sprayed on. By spraying with alternate constituent colours a brighter combination on the paper can be obtained than by mixing them together first in the wash. Settlement of the pigments in the wash must not take place or the colour of the spray will vary.

Air brush

For large and small areas and for fine and regular sprays there is nothing to surpass the air-brush, which is operated by compressed air (Fig. 10.28), although the expense is probably only justified when a considerable number of drawings are being dealt with continually. The compressed air is supplied from a cylinder charged by means of a foot-pump or electric compressor, through a rubber hose to the 'brush', which has a receptacle for ink, colour, etc., and a control button for varying the spray. With a little practice interesting and beautiful renderings can be carried out. The main danger to guard against is the somewhat 'artificial' air that the mechanical perfection

SPRAY SHOULD BE HORIZONTAL TO ALLOW HEAVY DROPS TO FALL CLEAR OF THE DRAWING.

JAR OF WASH AND SPRAYER TO BE HELD FIRMLY – WITH TUBE ALMOST AT BOTTOM OF JAR – AND MOVED SIMULTANEOUSLY.

SPRAY

Fig. 10.27

FINE WIRE MESH HELD A FEW INCHES ABOVE THE DRAWING

STIFF BRUSH

SPATTER

Fig. 10.26

SPRAY CONTROL

RECEPTACLE FOR WASH

COMPRESSED AIR SUPPLY TUBE

AIR BRUSH   *Fig. 10.28*

of the spray tends to give. Masks or templates have to be used as before, but drawings need not necessarily be vertical.

Transfer tones and colours

Various kinds of mechanical tones or tints, e.g. hatching and shadings, closely spaced lines, dots, and other patterns, can be applied to final drawings and tracing media by pressure transfer from standard paper-backed sheets of acetate film printed in black in a manner similar to the pressure transfer lettering described in Chapter 4. The usual procedure, however, is to place the selected sheet over the required area of the drawing with the backing paper underneath. Using a sharp knife, a piece of film slightly larger than the area is then cut out, care being taken not to cut the backing paper. The piece of film is removed from the backing sheet and is put in position and pressed gently onto the drawing. The surplus film is removed by cutting away or scraping; and finally the film is covered with paper and firmly burnished for positive adhesion. The adhesive is heat-resistant and the drawing can be safely reproduced by the dyeline process. Fig. 10.29 illustrates an example. The tones can be used to indicate shades and shadows, to distinguish plan areas, and to represent different materials, etc.

Matt and glossy colours can also be applied to final drawings by a similar technique, although the methods of application differ; the makers' current directions should be carefully followed.

Perspective rendering

The following notes on his personal method of rendering perspective drawings have been kindly supplied by Frank A. Evans.

'It is wise to employ a system that, barring accidents, will ensure success, and for this reason I use paper pre-mounted on boards rather than stretched paper to save time. I use a dry technique for the sky such as pastel, which can be manipulated more easily than water-colour. The use of a carbon pencil, not too soft, for line drawing reproduces well. It is not 'deadened' by water colour: that is, it shows through the colour. I also use opaque colours in moderation to emphasize focal points, foliage, etc. I consider it always essential to make an accurate setting up of perspectives in the first place.'

(Mr Evans' method of setting up perspectives is similar to that described earlier in this chapter.)

Presentation

There are so many ways of presenting rendered and all types of display drawing that only a brief guide can be given. Exhibitions, whether specifically architectural or of any kind of a graphic nature, provide examples and ideas that can be adopted, adapted or used to suggest new methods. The intention behind the presentation will influence its mode, which must be appropriate.

Presentation may involve added lettering, symbols, etc. Almost all presentation drawings, unless prepared on premounted paper, have to be mounted on stiff card or, if large, on hardboard, although lightness as well as rigidity for ease of handling and transport is a consideration. Slow-drying, non-penetrating pastes or spray adhesives are best for complete contact mounting as this enables the drawing to be manipulated into position and then smoothed out and made perfectly flat. This can be done by placing a sheet of tracing paper over it and then pushing hard with the edge of a scale or roller outwards from the centre to the edges to remove air bubbles and ridges. Care should be taken to avoid using too much adhesive.

The drawing thus mounted should be left on a horizontal surface, covered with a clean sheet of tracing paper and weighted down with evenly distributed piles of journals or books until dry. Subsequently, a cut-out surround can be added, with or without a border.

Alternatively, but more costly, drawings can be commercially mounted and, if required, framed and glazed.

However, drawings, whether mounted or not, can be readily protected by covering them with transparent self-adhesive film, which is obtainable in sheets and rolls. In addition to affording protection against the hazards of handling – and this applies particularly to drawings used in workshops or on construction sites – the film imparts brightness. The film comes with an 'easy-peel' removable backing printed with guide 'squares' for convenience of alignment and cutting and with instructions for application. There are two kinds of film: gloss for normal purposes and matt for use where lines in felt-tip pen or other media may have to be added. Relatively small drawings, if to be covered by film, can be affixed to card merely by arrowmounts.

Fig. 10.29 Application and examples of transfer hatchings and shadings for planning maps and architectural drawings. (Reproduced by permission of Letraset Ltd)

11
Freehand Drawing

The ability to make freehand drawings simply and quickly is of value to anyone: to architects, surveyors, planners and everybody connected with the design and construction of buildings. Freehand drawing is a way in which these professionals communicate their ideas. There is no better way of enjoying, remembering and understanding the built environment than to draw it. To keep a sketchbook of drawn impressions is an ideal way of investigating and analysing three-dimensional form and spaces. This type of informal drawing is essential in townscape evaluation, where drawn images of architectural style, character, proportion, scale and texture are important in analysing townscape quality. Freehand drawing is also useful for sketching building construction details as well as orthographic, isometric, axonometric and one- and two-point perspective.

Training in freehand drawing consists of (1) training the 'eye', including the 'mind's eye' or imagination, and (2) training the 'hand' to express what is seen.

The practice of sketching

Perhaps the best piece of advice to anyone upon sketching is that he or she does it. Sketching should be regarded as a pleasure as well as work. Sketching is both a means of expression and a method of analysis. However, although sketches may be a delight one should avoid mistaking the means for the ends. Sketches do but serve the art of building; 'to use them too much for ornament is affectation'.

A rapidly produced sketch can convey more information than many words. Surveyors, architects and town and countryplanners all need to be able to visualize their ideas through sketching.

The uses to which sketches are put vary from one professional discipline to another, but they generally have two main practical objectives:

- The allow thoughts relating to construction, scale, proportion and context to be clarified for the development of ides that may be described geometrically.
- They allow these ideas to be transmitted to others.

In other words, the sketch informs the sketcher as well as others interpreting the sketch.

Surveyors, architects and town and country planners are expected to be able to sketch as a way of communicating ideas quickly, confidently and clearly. This method of communicating ideas is the quickest and cheapest form, for now and future references not only with developers, contractors and clients, but with fellow professionals also.

Sketching can be done on paper of many kinds and sizes; tracing paper, cartridge paper, and various tinted papers. Soft pencils for 'finish lines' and harder pencils for 'construction lines' may also be used. Ink drawing pens give a more permanent line but are harder to erase.

The student should learn to appreciate *scale* as well as the use of different scales. The knowledge of orthographic projection is essential as well as isometric and axonometric projections.

Finally it should be remembered that it is not always necessary to produce expensive fully finished carefully presented ink drawings, either manually or by CAD. These have their place.

Training in freehand drawing consists of (1) training the 'eye', including the 'mind's eye' or imagination, and (2) training the 'hand' to express what is seen.

Elementary technique

In looking at a building or any object, or in imagining it, it is helpful to analyse it into (1) shapes bounded by lines, and (2) axes.

Whatever the sketch is to be – a plan, elevation, section, perspective – it can be resolved into its essential simple geometrical shapes, as seen in one plane.

At the same time, any prominent axial lines (lines of symmetry) can be noted. Almost every subject, whether strictly symmetrical or not, has axial lines of some kind or, failing these, outstanding horizontal or vertical lines. Such lines are the first to be drawn, and using them as a basis the various geometrical figures can be built up in correct proportion. When the skeleton of lines is complete, the most important features are sketched in, and after these the next important, and so on, to details as may be necessary. All the drawing is done in the first instance by lines; shades and shadows should be only if essential for the purposes of the sketch. By practice it will be found that a great deal can be expressed by straight, curved and squiggly lines and by dots, making further elaboration unnecessary.

Preliminary exercises _____

The majority of preliminary sketches are best made in pencil. The pencil should be fairly soft, well sharpened, and firm under pressure on smooth paper.

Straight lines

Fig. 11.1 illustrates examples that should be practised. All lines must be drawn freehand and must be as straight and even in quality as possible. A slight wobble is not serious, but there is no virtue in trying to make an irregular line.

1. Horizontal lines drawn from left to right. To help in keeping them horizontal try making them equidistant from the edge of the paper (use paper with straight square edges, it is easier). A line 50 mm long is good enough at first; longer lines can always be made up of a succession of short lines. After a single line has been drawn satisfactorily, draw several horizontal lines parallel and equally spaced to one another – all, of course, by eye.
2. Vertical lines drawn from top to bottom. Keep parallel to the side of the paper.
3. Lines at right angles. Draw either the horizontal or the vertical first, then the other to cross at right angles through a determined point.
4. Lines at 45°. First draw lines at 45° to pass in both directions through the intersection of lines at right angles drawn as in (3). Then try drawing 45° lines by themselves. Check for accuracy afterwards with set square.
5. Square. Drawn with horizontal and vertical lines, starting with different sides first. Check for accuracy.
6. Octagon. Drawn by adding 45° lines to square.
7. Lettering, patterns, etc., composed of straight lines.

   If it is found that the vertical lines persistently slant in one direction, try to correct the tendency by deliberately making such lines lean a little (as you see them) to the other side. If the difficulty is serious, vision is defective.

Curved lines

Fig. 11.2 illustrates examples.
1.2 Circle. Easiest way is to draw two lines lightly at right angles, mark on them points equally spaced from the intersection and draw the curve to pass through the points. The fullness of the curve will be assisted if the points are marked by short cross lines.

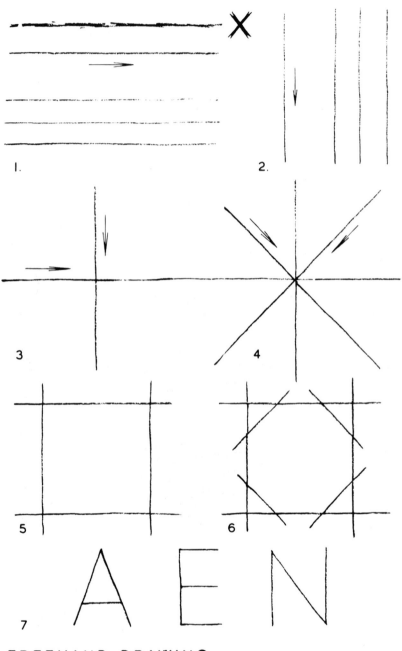

FREEHAND DRAWING
ELEMENTARY EXERCISES   STRAIGHT LINES

Fig. 11.1

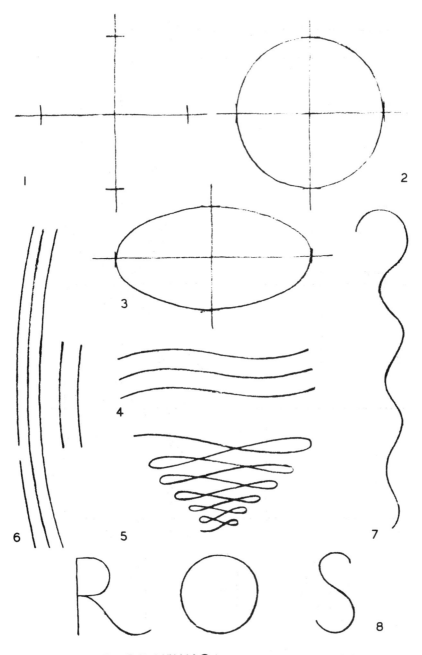

FREEHAND DRAWING
ELEMENTARY EXERCISES   *CURVED LINES*

Fig. 11.2

3. Ellipse. Similar procedure to circle.
4. Line of double curvature. Draw them to various sizes.
5. Continuous diminishing looped line. Practice for smoothness and regularity.
6. Flat arcs.
7. Free curves.
8. Lettering or simple pattern composed of curved or curved and straight lines.

When the above exercises have been practised and present no difficulty, then any building or object can be sketched provided the eye has been trained to pick out the essential lines.

Fig. 11.3 shows examples of the setting-up and finished sketches of a number of plans: (1) and (2) the plan of the house in Fig. 7.28. This consists of straight lines mainly at right-angles, as do most building plans. Note the 'filling-in' of walls; centre lines through openings, arrows at entrances, etc., all conventions to help legibility. (3) Plans of a Greek temple. Note drawing of line and marking of centres of columns in setting-up. (4) Bramante's plan for St. Peter's Church, Rome. Note the stages in the setting-up. In such an axial plan only one-quarter needs to be fully completed. (5) Irregular shape. Note representatin of water in pool and of grass by short dashes.

Fig. 11.4 shows examples of the setting-up and indication of elevations. (1) is the elevation of the house in Fig. 7.29, showing the main lines. (2) is a smaller thumb nail sketch of the same subject. (3) and (4) St Paul's, London. Note the setting-up of the main lines. The first line drawn is the ground line, then the vertical axes, then the main horizontal divisions. This sequence is suitable for most elevations. Note also the rapid suggestion of detail in the completed half of the sketch. (5) Sketch of a detail. Note how main shape and outline are established first, and the thickening of some lines to suggest form.

For most uses the above type of sketch is adequate, but a greater degree of finish can be given. By adding conventional shadows, by eye, the third dimension can be brought out more strongly, and the sketch passes from the diagrammatic to the semi-pictorial. By the addition of surroundings and an indication of material, texture, etc., attractive pictorial sketches can be made if necessary. All this is excellent practice for the development of a personal style of free sketching in which the preliminary stages are done automatically and the initial setting-up on paper is omitted, Fig. 11.5.

Freehand perspective

Perspective or metric freehand drawings can be made on exactly the same lines as described above for plans and elevations. There is no essential dif-

1
MAIN LINES

GROUND PLAN
2
FINISHED SKETCH

SIMPLE RECTANGULAR   NON-AXIAL

AXIS

PLAN OF THE
PARTHENON,
ATHENS.
3

AXIS

4 BRAMANTE'S
PLAN FOR
S. PETER'S,
ROME.

AXIAL

GRID OF STRAIGHT LINES
SUPERIMPOSED

TREES

WALL

GRASS

POOL

BUILDING

5

IRREGULAR   SHAPES

FREEHAND DRAWING
SETTING UP AND INDICATION OF PLANS

Fig. 11.3

1   ELEVATION

2   "THUMB-NAIL" SKETCH

3   FIRST STAGE IN SETTING UP MAIN LINES

MAIN LINES

GUIDE LINES

COMPLETED SKETCH WITH SHADE LINES TO SUGGEST FORM

5   ACANTHUS LEAF

4   COMPLETED SKETCH (DETAIL CAN BE OMITTED OR INCREASED AS REQUIRED)

WEST ELEVATION · St PAUL'S CATHEDRAL, LONDON.

FREEHAND DRAWING
SETTING UP AND INDICATION OF ELEVATIONS

Fig. 11.4

SEMI-PICTORIAL

PICTORIAL

FREEHAND DRAWING
RENDERING OF ELEVATIONS

Fig. 11.5

ference in technique. Good practice is obtained by drawing solids in various projections.

Fig. 11.6 illustrates certain points in connection with perspectives. The most important is that an eye-level (horizontal) on which must lie the vanishing points (see Chapter 9) must be established by trial or judgement to avoid distortion, although the construction need only be lightly indicated. It is a common mistake to have the vanishing points at different levels. The drawing of curved or more complex forms is made easier by enclosing them in 'boxes' or frameworks of straight lines.

Freehand perspectives can also be made on tracing paper, for subsequent photoprinting, over perspective grids, as described in Chapter 9.

It is possible to use a photocopier to either enlarge or reduce the size of freehand sketches. These sketches may then be mounted on a suitable paper-backing-sheet with additional annotation, if required and re-photocopied to produce, for example, a presentation sketchbook or a townscape appraisal.

Sketching mistakes on originals or photocopies may be eradicated by using a suitable white opaque correcting fluid such as Snowpake or Tipp-Ex. The sketch may be easily corrected once the fluid has dried, and the photocopying process removes all traces of any amendments.

If colour-rendered sketches are required, the original or the photocopy may be rendered either with water-colour pencils or with other suitable media, and further prints may be obtained using a laser colour copier.

Advanced freehand drawing

When reasonable facility in pencil drawing has been attained, the student can without difficulty pass to a variety of freehand techniques, ranging from loosely outlined design concepts to highly finished renderings of defined projects or subjects, including combinations of mechanical and freehand lines, applied tones and colours, etc., making use of whatever medium is best suited to the object of the drawing.

Personal preference will manifest itself in due course, and while some draughters may be versatile and have a facility In employing several techniques, others may tend to keep more or less to one distinctive style.

There are many very good books dealing with particular aspects of freehand drawing, and examples abound to assist and inspire. Some of these have been referred to in the foregoing text and some are listed in the references that follow.

Figs. 11.7–11.15 show examples of freehand and combined mechanical/freehand drawings with brief descriptive notes.

NORMAL
EYE-LEVEL

1.

2.   EYE-LEVEL ALONG GROUND

AN EYE-LEVEL (HORIZONTAL) AND
VANISHING POINTS MUST BE ESTAB-
LISHED BY TRIAL OR JUDGEMENT

EYE-LEVEL ABOVE OBJECT

3.

4.   ONE POINT PERSPECTIVE FOR
INTERIORS & VISTAS

DRAWING OF CURVED & MORE COMPLEX FORMS
MADE EASIER BY ENCLOSING THEM IN RECTANGULAR
"BOXES".

5.

6.

SKETCH PERSPECTIVE

Fig. 11.6

Fig. 11.7 Freehand drawing in black ink on white paper of rococo facade. The technique is admirably suited to the subject. (Norah R. Glover)

Carefully drawn design for a hotel interior. (Malcolm Read, MCSN, FSA1)

Fig. 11.8 Rapid freehand sketches of interior designs in ballpoint pen coloured by felt-tipped water-colour pens. (John F. Reekie)

Fig. 11.9 Careful freehand pen and black ink drawing on white card, combining variety of indications with strong unity of style and composition. Interest heightened by judicious use of sharp contrasts. Reproduced about quarter actual size. (F.A. Evans)

Fig. 11.10 Perspective sketch in pencil and ink of memorial chapel. (Design and drawing by Fraser Reekie)

LATER (GOTHIC) SPIRES

LATER 'CHEVET'

OCTAGONAL TOWER OVER CROSSING (OPEN ARCADING)

STEEPLY PITCHED ROOFS

CHARACTERISTIC ROMANESQUE VERTICAL STRIPS & CORBEL TABLING

ISOMETRIC

OUTLINE OF LATER ADDITIONS

APSE

OPEN ARCADING

E. APSIDAL CHAPEL

TRANSEPT

SEXPARTITE VAULTING OPEN NAVE

150 FEET.

PLAN
ABBAYE AUX HOMMES, CAEN, (AD. 1066)

WORMS CATHEDRAL - EAST END.

TRANSEPT

TOWER EASTERN APSE

DOMICAL QUADRI-PARTITE VAULTING

NAVE

TOWER

WESTERN APSE

TOWER

TOWER

PLAN
WORMS CATHEDRAL (AD 1110-1200)

WALL ARCHES

DIAGONAL RIBS

TRANSVERSE RIB

DIAGRAM SEXPARTITE VAULT

SCULPTURED TYMPANUM

FIGURES OF SAINTS

COLUMNS ON CARVED LIONS

ENTRANCE PORCH (DETAILS BASED ON ROMAN WORK)

French & German Romanesque

S. TROPHÎME, ARLES (AD 1150)

Fig. 11.11 Architectural history sketches in pen and ink over pencil guidelines.

Fig. 11.12 Black pencil sketch over some lightly ruled guidelines set up on site by eye. Note effective use of dark, graded shadows. An excellent example of pencil technique. Reproduced abaout half actual size. (F.A. Evans)

Fig. 11.13   Example of a quick sketch made on site using felt-tip pen on ordinary loose-leaf pad paper. A simple but effective technique for various architectural and planning study purposes. Reproduced about half actual size. (Tony McCarthy)

Fig. 11.14   Black ink drawing using Rotrary Rapid 0.25 and 0.35 liner pens on white paper. Example of carefully observed freehand drawing to show architectural detail. (The Furret Room, St. Matthias College, Bristol, by P. E. Dyke)

Fig. 11.15   Example of careful feehand drawing on paper to show house and garden details (Technique as in **Fig. 11.14**; by P. E. Dyke)

References

In addition to the references in the text, the following publications are sources of further technical information on the preparation of various kinds of drawing.

BS 1192 *Construction Drawing Practice*
    Part 1: 1984 *Recommendations for general principles*
    Part 2: 1987 *Recommendations for architectural and engineering drawings*
    Part 3: 1987 *Recommendations for symbols and other graphic conventions*
    Part 4: 1984 *Recommendations for landscape drawings*
    Part 5: 1990 *Guide for structuring of computer graphic information*
Burden E. *Architectural Delineation A Photographic Approach*. New York: McGraw-Hill, 1971
Carson G.S. *Computer Graphics*. Vol 27, No 2, September 1993.
Carson G.S (ed.) *Introduction to the Computer Graphics Model. Computer Graphics*. Vol 27, No 2, September 1993.
Crosley M.L. *The Architect's Guide to Computer Aided Design*. New York: John Wiley, 1988.
Development Plans: A Manual of Form and Content. London: HMSO 1970
Doyle M.E. *Color Drawing*. New York: Van Nostrand Reinhold
Halse A.O. *Architectural Rendering*. New York: McGraw-Hill, 1960
Jacoby H. *New Architectural Drawings*. London: Thames & Hudson, 1969
Jacoby H. *New Techniques of Architectural Rendering*. London: Thames and Hudson, 1971.
Kautzky T. *Ways With Water Color*. New York: Reinhold, 1949
Porter T., Greenstreet B. *Manual of Graphic Techniques 1 for Architects, Graphic Designers and Artists*. New York: Charles Scribner's Sons, 1983
Ray-Jones A., McCann W. *CI/SfB Project Manual*. London: Architectural Press.
RIBA Handbook of Architectural Practice and Management. London: Royal Institute of British Architects, 1991: section 3410.
The Detailing of Reinforced Concrete. London: Concrete Society/Institution of Structural Engineers.
Weddle A.E. *Techniques of Landscape Architecture*. London: Heinemann, 1967.

Working Drawings. BRE Digest 172. Garston: Building Research Establishment, 1974

To keep abreast of changes and developments such periodicals as Architects/Journal, *Architectural Review*, RIBA Journal, *Building Design, The Planner* Journal of the Royal Town Planning Institute, *Journal of the Institute of Landscape Architects*, and similar publications are a useful source. The bookshop of the Royal Institute of British Architects is a rich source of new material on graphic and related techniques. Also the librarians of the major professional institutes will usually assist in locating relevant material on any particular aspect of draughting and drawing.

Index